Indiana Miscellany:
Consisting of
Sketches of Indian Life,
The Early Settlements,
Customs and Hardships of the People,
And
The Introduction of
The Gospel and of Schools;
Together with Biographical Notices
Of
The Pioneer Methodist Preachers
Of the State

Rev. William C. Smith

HERITAGE BOOKS
2008

HERITAGE BOOKS
AN IMPRINT OF HERITAGE BOOKS, INC.

Books, CDs, and more—Worldwide

For our listing of thousands of titles see our website at
www.HeritageBooks.com

Published 2008 by
HERITAGE BOOKS, INC.
Publishing Division
100 Railroad Ave. #104
Westminster, Maryland 21157

Copyright © 1867, 2002 Rev. William C. Smith

All rights reserved. No part of this book may be reproduced or transmitted in any form or by any means, electronic or mechanical, including photocopying, recording or by any information storage and retrieval system without written permission from the author, except for the inclusion of brief quotations in a review.

International Standard Book Numbers
Paperbound: 978-0-7884-2229-4
Clothbound: 978-0-7884-7300-5

TO

The Descendants

OF

THE EARLY SETTLERS OF INDIANA,

This Volume

IS

RESPECTFULLY DEDICATED,

BY

THE AUTHOR.

PREFACE.

In the following pages I have not presumed to write a *history*, but simply sketches and incidents of the early settlement of Indiana, and of some of the noble men and women who first emigrated to her territory. Much of what I have written has been from memory and personal knowledge.

I have desired to rescue from oblivion some incidents in the history of my native State, and perpetuate the memory of some of the worthy pioneers who endured all the hardships and privations of a frontier life.

I have presented a brief sketch of the introduction of Methodism into Indiana. I would, with pleasure, have given some account of the introduction of other Christian denominations into the State if I had been in possession of the proper data to enable me to do so. Some of them have acted a noble part in spreading the "savor of a Redeemer's name" in Indiana.

I have not attempted to give a sketch of any

living man—only those who have passed away. There are others who are worthy to be had in remembrance. Perhaps an abler pen will perpetuate their memory.

Doubtless imperfections and inaccuracies will be discovered if the following pages are subjected to a critical examination; nevertheless, I hope the reader will find some entertainment. Each chapter is designed to be complete of itself, and may be perused to suit the convenience of the reader. Hoping to find some favor, I send this volume to the public.

WM. C. SMITH.

MARTINSVILLE, IND., 1867.

CONTENTS.

CHAPTER I.
First Settling of Indiana—Vincennes—The Indians—Early Hardships and Privations—Structure of the Cabins—How Fortified—Indian Traits—Incidents—Killbuck..........................Pages 14–23

CHAPTER II.
Eastern Indiana—The Pigeon-Roost Massacre of 1812—Persons Killed—A Sugar-Camp Massacre—The Hudson Family—Horrible Atrocities—An Incident—The Settlers Subject to Perpetual Fears—An Indian Monster—Sources of Enjoyment...........................24–34

CHAPTER III.
Introduction of Schools—School-Houses; how made—Rules for Punishments—Playing-Spells and Kinds of Sports—New Testament a Text-Book—Difficulties in Obtaining Teachers.......................35–38

CHAPTER IV.
Morals of the People—The First Murder in all the Eastern Part of the State—Criss the Murderer—The Execution—Throngs of People.. 39–42

CHAPTER V.
The Introduction of the Gospel among the First Settlers—The Sabbath; how spent—What Methodist Itinerancy has done for the State—The Preachers and their Qualifications—A "Son of Thunder" at a Camp Meeting—The Women Gifted in Prayer.........43–48

CHAPTER VI.
Introduction of Methodism—Whitewater the name of the First Circuit—Its Extent—Joseph Williams and John Sell—Church Sta-

8 CONTENTS.

tistics—Various Preachers and their Fields of Labor—Vincennes—Anecdote of General Harrison—Additional Circuits Formed—Mr. Axley and Bishop Morris—Old Western Conference Divided—Further Statistics..Pages 49–61

CHAPTER VII.

Meeting-Houses—Meetings in the Cabins and Groves—Process of Building the Primitive Churches—Carr's Meeting-House—Methodist Church in Wayne County—Men who Preached in it—Fine Churches—The First Methodist Meeting-House in Indiana—Salem the Third Meeting-House—First Frame Church Erected—Labors of Rev. James Havens in Securing Subscriptions......................62–70

CHAPTER VIII.

Camp Meetings—Character of the Worship and Services—The Closing Exercises—The First Camp Meeting held—Rev. Hugh Cull..71–75

CHAPTER IX.

Further Sketches and Incidents—The War of 1812-13—Block Houses—Hazards of Hunting—The Women of Those Days—Their Skill with the Rifle—An Incident—Miss Patsey Odell and her Night Adventure...76–83

CHAPTER X.

Christopher Roddy—His Frightful Wickedness—Challenged to Fight—A Ridiculous End—Pitt, a Colored Man, and Roddy's Promise to him...84–88

CHAPTER XI.

Three Friends—Death of the youngest—Death of a second one—His Disturbance in Mind—Lingering Illness and Death of the third—Solemn Warnings..89–93

CHAPTER XII.

George Julian—Early Training—Love of Adventure—His Qualities as a Singer, Class-Leader, etc.—A Sorrowful Experience—His Death...94–97

CONTENTS.

CHAPTER XIII.

Methodist Exhorters and their Services—Scarcity of Preachers—Hardy Cain—James Honley—Spencer—John Doddridge.Pages 98-103

CHAPTER XIV.

Moral Heroines—The Women Not Ashamed or Afraid to Pray—Their Attendance at Quarterly and Protracted Meetings—Nearly All Passed Away..104-106

CHAPTER XV.

Progress of Methodism in the State—1819—Placing of the Circuits—Calvin Ruter and other preachers—Number of Circuits in 1823—Increase of Members and general aspect of Methodism...107-117

CHAPTER XVI.

Politics—Caucuses and Conventions unknown things—No Democrats, Whigs, or Republicans—Election Days—Stump Speeches—The Raccoon and the Rooster as insignia—When and Why Adopted—Joseph Chapman and Thomas Walpole—The "Ruffled-Shirt Gentry"—A Shrewd Trick of Walpole's...................117-124

CHAPTER XVII.

Mrs. Sarah Smith—Early Left an Orphan—Her Nobility of Character—Unites with the Methodist Episcopal Church—The Inoree River Valley Camp Meeting—Gifted in Prayer—Blessing of Perfect Love—The War of 1812-13—Construction of Forts—Mrs. Smith's Death 125-134

CHAPTER XVIII.

George Smith—Birthplace—Death of Both his Parents—Marriage—Conversion—Emigrates to the West—A Faithful Reader of the Holy Scriptures—Last Days and Death—His Children....135-144

CHAPTER XIX.

Rev. Moses Crume—His Awakening and Conversion—His Appointments—Personal Appearance—His Piety—Death.................145-147

CONTENTS.

CHAPTER XX.

Rev. John Strange—Admitted on Trial 1811—A Virginian by birth—First Appointment—Indian Troubles—A Characteristic Incident—Formation of the Illinois Conference—Personal Appearance—Eccentricities—Power as a Preacher—Death .... Pages 148-156

CHAPTER XXI.

Rev. Hugh Cull—Roman Catholic Parentage—Comes to Indiana—His Physical Frame—His Preaching Abilities—Last Days..... 157-161

CHAPTER XXII.

Rev. John Gibson—Early Education—A Terror to Evil-Doers—His Zeal and Piety—An Incident 162-164

CHAPTER XXIII.

Introduction of Methodism into Richmond—The "Friends" not friendly to the New Religion—A Two Days' Meeting—A Time of Power—An Incident—Mr. Henry—A New Church—Rev. Mr. Baughman Warned—Happy Termination 165-176

CHAPTER XXIV.

Steadfastness of a Pious Wife—Rev. S. R. Beggs—Mrs. H.—Her Husband and His Wickedness—The Wife's Perplexities and Troubles—A Love-Feast—Conversion of Mr. H 177-184

CHAPTER XXV.

Rev. Russel Bigelow—His Early Life—Admission into the Traveling Connection—Personal Knowledge of the Scriptures—An Anecdote—His Eloquence—His Manners and Habits—His Mighty Faith 185-195

CHAPTER XXVI.

Rev. Allen Wiley—A Virginian by birth—Early Opportunities—His Studies—A Hater of Pedantry—His Personal Appearance—As a Pastor and Preacher—Extent of his Labors 196-205

CHAPTER XXVII.

Rev. Nehemiah B. Griffith—His Conversion—Various Appointments—His Death—His Faithfulness—Ability as a Preacher.. 206-209

CONTENTS. 11

CHAPTER XXVIII.

The Young Lawyer—His First Effort at Early Culture—His Marriage—His Death-bed Experience and Confessions......Pages 210-223

CHAPTER XXIX.

James Epperson—A Bit of the Author's Experience—A Sad Story—A Consultation—Weariness of Body and Gloom of Mind—A Happy Dissipation—Rare Nobility of Character Displayed—An Incident—Epperson's Early Life—His Gifts........................224-235

CHAPTER XXX.

Hon. James Rariden—Early Life—Intellectual Powers—An Active Politician and Jurist—His Large-Heartedness—A Story for Stingy People...236-241

CHAPTER XXXI.

An Eccentric Circuit Steward—Neglecting Class Meeting—A Reason Assigned—Quarterage—Paying Up...........................242-245

CHAPTER XXXII.

Rev. L. W. Berry, D. D.—Born in Vermont—W. B. Christie—Berry as a Student—A Camp Meeting Incident—First Sermon—Marriage—A Debate—Universalism—Different Appointments—President of Indiana Asbury University—His Term of Service—Resignation—Goes to Iowa—Thence to Missouri—Death—His Characteristics—Tribute to his Memory..................................246-263

CHAPTER XXXIII.

Rev. James Havens—Early Life—Marriage—Conversion—Enters the Ministry—Various Appointments—His Labors—An Incident of Early Life—One of his Ministry—A Third—Peculiarities—Power in Prayer—As a Conductor of Camp Meetings—Modes of Fighting Satan—His Mental Powers—Ability as a Preacher—Illness and Death... 264-285

CHAPTER XXXIV.

Rev. Isaac Owen—Born in Vermont—Death of his Father—Early Educational Opportunities Limited—As a Preacher—One of the Endowment Agents of Indiana Asbury University—Goes to California—Personal Appearance—His Illness and Death.............Pages 286-292

CHAPTER XXXV.

Edward Brown—Marriage—Conversion—As a Church Officer—A Request concerning his own Funeral—Sickness and Death.....293-298

CHAPTER XXXVI.

Rev. Calvin W. Ruter—Early Life in Obscurity—Received on Trial in Ohio Conference 1818—Samuel Hamilton—A Pentecostal Camp Meeting—Frail Health—Member of the General Conference of 1844—Personal Appearance—Preaching Abilities—His Pathos—His Death.. 299-304

INDIANA MISCELLANY.

CHAPTER I.

FIRST SETTLING OF INDIANA.

SIXTY-SIX years ago what is now the great State of Indiana was almost one unbroken wilderness. Here and there, in the southern and southeastern portions, a settler had broken the forest and erected his rude log cabin, and a few towns had been laid out.

Vincennes, on the Wabash River, was an old French post which had been settled sometime between 1700 and 1735. Those who have written on the subject differ as to the time. The probabilities are it was settled as early as 1710. None fix the period later than 1735. Those who desire more particular information upon this subject will find it in "Western Annals," by James H. Perkins. For many years this was the solitary spot in the vast wilderness inhabited by civilized man. The French who had fixed their habitation here, so far from civilization, by their intercourse with the Indians, soon became very much assimilated into the manners and customs of their savage life. It could not for many years, therefore, hardly be called any thing more than a town of half-savages. All middle and northern Indiana was one wild wilderness, where the red man roamed over hills and valleys free; none to dispute his right save the wild beasts which sometimes contended with him for the mastery—for a habitation with him in their native forests. The Indian felt himself to be Lord of the soil. He looked upon the vast herds of deer and buffalo, and the numerous flocks of turkies, pheasants, and prairie-hens as all his own, given to him by the Great Spirit for the sustenance of himself, his squaw, and his pappooses; and the bear, wolf, otter, beaver, and raccoon as so many instrumentalities furnished to his hand in order that he might have raiment with which to keep warm during the long months of dreary Winter.

Hunting and trapping were his delight. In taking his game he felt that he was taking his own as much as the inhabitants of the State do now when they go into their fields and meadows to slaughter their fat cattle, or into their barnyards to obtain poultry for their tables. It is not much to be wondered at, then, that when the white man came and began to take of his flocks and herds, and clear away the forest, and thereby spoil his hunting-ground, that the red man should feel that he was being seriously wronged, and that the spirit of revenge should arise in his bosom. Savage though he was, a native of the wild-woods, having no knowledge of civilization, he had, nevertheless, some idea of justice—of right. To see what he believed to be his own taken from him by another not of his kindred, tongue, or people, made him feel that the wrong was *too* great to be submitted to—an outrage not to be borne without resistance and struggle; hence the bloody wars between the white and the red man—the unnumbered massacres of men, women, and children. Would white men, with all their boasted civilization, have submitted to such a flagrant violation of what they considered their rights?—such an appropriation of their lands and personal property to the benefit of another—a people of another race?

But the Indian has gone—gone further toward the setting sun. Though once they roamed through every forest in Indiana, and their camp-fires were burning on every hill-top and in every valley, and their wild whoop heard to ring in all the forest, they have all disappeared, save a few who still cling to the graves of their fathers. Instead of the wild, unbroken forests which stood in all their majestic grandeur sixty-six years ago, now, in every part of Indiana, fields of golden grain are seen; instead of the wigwam, the stately farm-house shows its proportions; instead of nature's orchards where grew the wild plum, cherry, and grape, now may be seen cultivated orchards, producing all the varieties of the most delicious fruits; instead of the Indian village, composed of a few smoky huts, now rises the populous city with its paved or macadamized streets, its extensive business-houses, stately mansions, and church edifices with their lofty spires pointing toward the clouds; instead of the narrow Indian trace the eye catches the track of the railway, along which dashes the iron-horse, hitched to the ponderous train containing its hundreds of human beings, or its many tuns of freight. How great the change sixty-six years have wrought!

The first settlers of Indiana were subjected to hardships, privations, and toils to which the present inhabitants are entire strangers. They were shut up to their own resources for the means of living and the necessaries of life. With all their energy, ingenuity, and skill these were few. They were inhabitants of the wilderness. Saw-mills, grist-mills, dry goods, and grocery stores were not in the country. Their cabins were built of unhewn logs covered with clapboards, stick and clay chimneys, with puncheon floors. Few of the cabins of the first settlers had a window in them. The reasons were two: first, there was no such thing as obtaining window-sash or window-glass; second, a window left an opening by which wild animals could enter, to the dismay of the family. Wolves, bears, panthers and wild-cats often prowled around their dwellings in the darkness of the night, to the great annoyance and terror of the family, particularly the little folks.

During the day the door of the cabin was kept open to afford light, and at night, through the Winter season, light was emitted from the fireplace, where huge logs were kept burning. Candles and lamps were out of the question for a few years. When these came into use, they were purely domestic in their manufacture. Candles were prepared by taking a wooden rod some ten or twelve inches in length, wrapping a strip of cotton or linen cloth around it, then covering it with tallow pressed on with the hand. These "sluts," as they were sometimes called, answered the purpose of a very large candle, and afforded light for several nights. Lamps were prepared by dividing a large turnip in the middle, scraping out the inside quite down to the rind, then inserting a stick, say three inches in length in the center, so that it would stand upright. A strip of cotton or linen cloth was then wrapped around it, and melted lard or deer's tallow was poured in till the turnip rind was full, then the lamp was ready for use. By the light of these, during the long Winter evenings, the women spun and sewed, and the men read, when books could be obtained. When neither lard nor tallow could be obtained, the large blazing fire supplied the needed light. By these great fireplaces many cuts of thread have been spun, many a yard of linsey woven, many a frock and pair of buckskin pantaloons made.

For several years there were no physicians among

the settlers. Medicines from an apothecary shop were not to be had. The people gathered their remedies from the woods and prairies, and administered them to themselves, without the formula of a prescription. A death was a rare occurrence in those days. When one did occur it produced a sensation among the people for miles around. All turned out to a funeral, though it was that of a little child.

Usually one man in each neighborhood served the people in the way of drawing teeth and bloodletting. There were no post-offices or post routes. Letters were conveyed by private hand. When the friends left behind in the older portions of the country desired to send a letter to those who had emigrated to Indiana, they were forwarded by some emigrant going further west, and addressed in something like the following: "To Mr. A. B., Whitewater Settlement of Friends, Indiana Territory." Instead of being directed to a post-office, letters were always directed to some particular settlement.

In addition to all the other hardships to which the first settlers were subjected, they had to contend with the hostile Indians. From the serious wrongs, as they considered, done them by the whites, wrongs they had been suffering for years, they became the sworn, inveterate foe of the "pale-faces." They had seen themselves driven back further and further toward the setting sun. Many of their tribes had become extinct. Around their camp-fires and in their wigwams they had talked over their grievances till, overborne by a sense of wrong, they had sworn eternal hatred and revenge against the white man.

Though sons of the forest, born and reared in the wild woods, they were keen, shrewd men, full of cunning, true to a friend, but deceitful and implacable toward an enemy. They were to the whites a dangerous and much-dreaded foe. The only thing that kept them from slaying the whites or carrying them off as prisoners when and wherever they came across them, was fear of being overpowered. The settlers never knew when to trust them. They were always in more or less dread day and night, hence it was necessary for them to be perpetually on their guard, well armed, and prepared for any emergency.

In this work of preparation for attacks the first settlers fortified their cabins as well as they could. The loft, as it was called, was constructed of split logs, so that an entrance could not be made from above. The doors were made of split timbers, from three to four inches in thickness, pinned firmly to battens, and hung upon strong wooden hinges running the whole width of the door. The fastening was made by boring a large augur-hole through on either side of the door, near the door cheek. Then the crotch of a limb was obtained from a forest tree, one prong of which was cut to a length of three or four inches, while the other was shaved to fit the augur hole. It was then driven in and wedged on the outside. When the door was shut a large wooden bar was dropped into the crotches; thus the door was fastened securely. The door-shutter was of such a thickness the Indians could not split it down with their tomahawks, and the bar in the inside held it so firmly it could not be forced open. The nights of the early boyhood of the writer were spent in a cabin thus secured.

There were some traits of character in the wild Indians peculiar to themselves. They always moved in single file, whether on foot or mounted; this habit gave rise to the phrase, "Indian file." We have seen hundreds of them thus traveling, stretching along the trace for miles. They had a peculiar whoop by which they made communications along the line when desired. The whoop given by one would be caught up and repeated as it ran along the line, till the forest would ring with hundreds of voices at one time.

When the Indians, in large or small companies, met a white person in the way, every one of them would instantly place his gun behind him, as if to conceal it from view. When they visited the cabins of the white people they invariably came up in the rear. Usually the settler's cabin had but one door. An Indian approaching would leave the path which led up in front and seek the rear, then walk along as stealthily as possible till the cabin was

FIRST SETTLING.   21

reached, when, suddenly springing round to the door, he would give his salute, thus, if possible, taking the family by surprise. It often happened that the first thing the family would know, five, ten, twenty, or more Indians, with guns, tomahawks, and scalping-knives were at the door. This habit of theirs kept the families of the settlers in almost perpetual dread.

The Indians had a great dislike to a coward. They admired a brave. It was unfortunate for the whites, if, when the Indians visited their cabins, they showed any signs of fear. If they did, they were very likely to have trouble before their visitors left. Seeing the fear of the white people they would menace them with their tomahawks and scalping-knives for the purpose of increasing their alarm. When the whites were well frightened they would take whatever they desired and appropriate it to their own use. It was necessary for the settlers, when the Indians came to their cabins or they met them in the way, to exhibit a bold and defiant spirit, however in mind and heart they might feel.

The writer recollects well, one night in midwinter, after the family had all retired to bed, that a very noted Indian, whose English name was Killbuck, came to the door of his father's cabin, and in broken English demanded admittance. The door being well barred, no answer was given. The demand was repeated several times, and still no answer. Finally, Killbuck struck the door several severe blows with his tomahawk, swearing he would split it down if it was not opened. My father then told him, in positive terms, if he did not leave immediately he would put a rifle-ball through him. Killbuck said he was cold and hungry, and wanted to warm and get something to eat. Fearing he was under the influence of liquor, he having just come from a trading-house a few miles below where whisky was kept to sell to the Indians, and that it would not be safe to let him in, he was told to go up the branch a short distance to where Old Sal, an Indian squaw, was camped, then come back in the morning, when he should have something to eat. After a time he left, declaring he would have one white man's scalp before morning. Early the next morning Killbuck returned in a fine humor. Approaching the writer's father, he said: "White man heap much brave; he no coward."

We give another incident: One day a number of Indians visited a settler's cabin to purchase some provisions. The settler was from home. Among other things they desired some bacon. The settler's wife went into the smoke-house to procure it. Several squaws followed her in. One of them took a large piece of bacon and started out. She was told she could not have that piece. The squaw persisted in carrying it off. The white woman seized the piece of meat, wrested it from the squaw, and struck her a blow which came near prostrating her. This caused great merriment among the Indians. The men gathered around the settler's wife, and patting her on the shoulder, said: "White squaw heap much brave; heap much fight."

In selling any thing to the Indians for money, it was difficult to obtain a fair price. In such a trade they were shrewd, but in bartering for their furs, peltries, baskets, moccasins, and broaches, they seemed to have little judgment. One so disposed could take great advantage of them. Mr. C., a white man, who had established a trading-house far out in the Indian country, having just received a supply of needles, told the Indians that the needle-maker was dead, and when what supply he had on hand was gone they would get no more. The result was he exchanged his needles each for a coonskin, when the skin was worth from fifty to seventy-five cents.

CHAPTER II.

FIRST SETTLING OF INDIANA, (CONTINUED.)

In Eastern Indiana the first settlers did not suffer as much from depredations by the Indians as in the southern portion of the territory. A terrible slaughter of the whites occurred in what is now Scott county, at a place near where the Jeffersonville & Indianapolis Railroad now passes, called the "Pigeon-Roost Massacre." I subjoin from "Dillon's History of Indiana" the following account of it:

"Within the present limits of the county of Scott, there was, in 1812, a place that was called 'The Pigeon-Roost Settlement.' This settlement, which was founded by a few families in 1809, was confined to about a square mile of land, and it was separated from all other settlements by a distance of five or six miles.

"In the afternoon of the 3d of September, 1812, Jeremiah Payne and a man whose name was Coffman, who were hunting for 'bee-trees' in the woods about two miles north of the 'Pigeon-Roost Settlement,' were surprised and killed by a party of Indians. This party of Indians, which consisted of ten or twelve warriors, nearly all of whom were Shawanees, then attacked the 'Pigeon-Roost Settlement' about sunset on the evening of the 3d of September, and in the space of about one hour killed one man, five women, and sixteen children. The bodies of some of these victims of savage warfare were burned in the fires which consumed the cabins in which the murders were perpetrated.

"The persons who were massacred at this settlement were: Henry Collings and his wife; Mrs. Payne, wife of Jeremiah Payne, and eight of her children; Mrs. Richard Collings and seven of her children; Mrs. John Morril and her only child, and Mrs. Morril, the mother of John Morril. Mrs. Jane Biggs, with her three small children, escaped from the settlement, eluded the vigilance of the Indians, and about an hour before daylight on the next morning arrived at the house of her brother, Zebulon Collings, who lived about six miles from the scene of carnage. William Collings, who had passed the age of sixty years, defended his house for the space of three-quarters of an hour against the attacks of the Indians. In this defense he was assisted by Captain John Norris. There were two children in the house. As soon as it began to grow dark, Mr. Collings and Captain Norris escaped with the two children, John Collings and Lydia Collings, from the house, eluded the pursuit of the Indians, and on the morning of the next day reached the house of Zebulon Collings.

"A number of the militia of Clark county immediately proceeded to the scene of the 'Pigeon-

Roost' massacre, where they found several of the mangled bodies of the dead, surrounded by the smoking ruins of the houses. The remains of the murdered persons were brought together and buried in one grave."

A man by the name of Shortrige was killed and scalped by the Indians, not far from where Cambridge City, Wayne county, now stands. Charles Morgan and two boys by the name of Beesly were killed by them at a sugar-camp, in what is now the north-western part of Wayne county. The Indians stealthily approached the camp where Morgan and the two boys were boiling sugar-water after night, and suddenly rushed upon them. Morgan made a powerful resistance, but was overpowered, and fell beneath the blows of their tomahawks. One of the boys was also killed with the tomahawk; the other started to run, but was shot a short distance from the camp. They also shot Morgan's dog.

Jonathan Shaw, who was boiling sugar-water at a camp not far away, hearing the Indian whoop, the fierce barking of Morgan's dog, and the report of two guns, knew that Morgan's camp was attacked by Indians. He immediately fled to the settlement and gave the alarm. The next day men went out and gathered up the dead bodies. They found Morgan terribly mutilated; the ax with which he had tried to defend himself lay near by, with marks of blood on it, indicating he had given his assailants some severe wounds. The boy that had been tomahawked was lying in the fire, partly consumed. The other boy they found a short distance from the camp, where he had fallen, having been shot as he ran. The three had been scalped. Morgan left a wife and four children. The boys left a widowed mother and one brother. This occurrence created great alarm among the settlers, and caused them to gather their families into the fort which they had erected for their protection.

About the year 1811, a family by the name of Hudson, who lived on the north side of Busaron creek, some distance above Fort Knox, on the Wabash River, were all murdered or taken prisoners and carried off by the Indians, except Mr. Hudson. The family consisted of Mr. and Mrs. Hudson, some five or six children, and a young man who lived with them. On the morning of this dreadful tragedy Mr. Hudson left home to attend to some business at Fort Knox, the young man went hunting, and Mrs. Hudson put her wash-kettle over the fire preparatory to washing. Some time after nightfall the following evening, Mr. Hudson was returning, and when within about one mile of his home his faithful dog met him and set up a most piteous howl. This strange conduct on the part of the dog caused him to have the most fearful apprehensions that some calamity had befallen his family. He hastened on as fast as possible. When he came in sight of his cabin he saw that it had been consumed by fire. He rode up to the smoldering ruins, but saw nothing of his family. He called them, but no answer came. As he rode round his ruined habitation his horse suddenly stopped and snorted. Looking a little way in advance, he saw the young man who belonged to his family lying dead, scalped, his heart torn out and lying upon his breast. Mr. Hudson believed this to be the work of Indians, and the dreadful thought flashed upon him that his family had been murdered by them or carried into captivity. He rode back to Fort Knox and reported what had been done. The next day a detachment of men were sent out from the Fort to the scene of the massacre. On arriving at the desolate home of Mr. Hudson they found the body of the young man as Mr. H. had seen it the night before. They found the body of the youngest child, an infant a few months old, in the kettle which Mrs. Hudson had hung over the fire the morning before, together with a few garments partly consumed, the back wall of the chimney having fallen upon them, but nothing could be found of Mrs. Hudson and the other children. It was supposed, that, when the Indians came to the cabin, finding Mrs. H. washing, they took her infant child and put it into the kettle of boiling clothes. They then made the mother and the other children prisoners, set fire to the house, and waited the return of the husband and father. When the young man came in from hunting, supposing him to be Mr. H., they attempted to take him prisoner, but he fought so desperately—for there were signs of a terrible conflict between him and the savages—they killed him and left his body, mutilated as it was found, and made off with Mrs. H. and her children. They were never heard of afterward.

Mr. Hudson, that he might have a better opportunity to avenge the destruction of his family by these savage fiends, joined a company of Rangers, but soon after was killed by the Indians in the prairie not far from where the city of Terre Haute now stands.

These wild savages seemed to have some idea of the old Mosaic law, "An eye for an eye, and a tooth for a tooth," for in their intercourse with the different tribes and with the whites they acted on it as a cardinal principle. If one of their number was slain by one of another nation or tribe, that nation or tribe must deliver up one of their number to be slain by them. They demanded the observance of this rule by the whites. If their demand was not granted they took vengeance till sated in their own way. In such an event, they would take two or three lives for one.

In the first settling of what is now Wayne county, the following incident occurred near the present site of the city of Richmond: A man by the name of Jones had been out hunting. On returning home he found an Indian at his cabin who had terribly frightened Mrs. Jones by his savage menaces, and was helping himself to whatever he desired. When Jones entered his cabin the Indian rushed out and made off as fast as he could run. Jones shot him as he ran, inflicting a severe, though not mortal, wound. The Indian made his escape and reached his people. This created great excitement among both Indians and whites. In a few days a delegation of Indians came into the white settlement and demanded redress for this shooting by Jones. The whites were so well acquainted with the Indian character that they knew some settlement of the difficulty must be made, or the Indians would take merciless vengeance—perhaps some of their women and children would be the sacrifice. Accordingly a council was called of all the men of the settlement. After some time spent in consultation, they appointed Esquire Rue, William L. Williford, and George Smith as commissioners to treat with the Indians and settle the difficulty. These commissioners met the Indian delegation. The Indians demanded *blood* from a white man. The commissioners pleaded that the wounded Indian had been the aggressor. In view of this fact the Indians proposed to take a horse. The commissioners agreed to give one. Accordingly they purchased a horse and handed him over to the Indians, and here the matter rested.

The inhabitants of Indiana at the present day, surrounded with all the blessings of civilization, can not realize the privations and sufferings endured by those who, with stout hearts and strong arms, entered the wilderness, broke the forest, plowed the soil, planted the first grain, made "the desert to rejoice and blossom as the rose," and laid the foundations, deep and broad, for her present prosperity and greatness. "One man soweth and another reapeth." It is equally true that one generation soweth and another reapeth.

Though the first settlers were brave, stout-hearted men and women, the dangers surrounding them were such, as already intimated, as to keep them in perpetual dread. Hundreds and thousands of Indians were constantly passing through the country. They were the most deadly foes of the white people. Many of them had grown old in blood-shedding. Many of the depredations committed upon the first settlers of Kentucky were by Indians from what is now the State of Indiana. At their village called Old Town, situated in what is now Delaware county, some five miles from Muncie, and near White River, many white men were tortured to death at the stake by a slow fire, while their fiendish captors danced around them. The writer visited that spot after the Indians had left the village, and saw the stake still standing, around which, at a short distance, the terrible fires had been kindled for the burning of the wretched victims captured by them. The stake was of oak, and was some ten feet high. At about the hight of a tall man, the rough outline of a human face had been cut on each side. The fires had been kindled in a circle around the stake at the distance of some five or six feet. These had been built so often that the ashes had formed a perceptible ridge. When we visited the place some of the firebrands were yet to be seen. Where the Indians had danced the ground was packed so hard that nothing would grow. Outside this circle, vegetation was luxuriant. We will not attempt to describe the feelings we had, nor the thoughts that crowded our mind as we stood there, musing, nor attempt to recall how many white persons had suffered a death too horrible to contemplate.

The writer recollects well of hearing an Indian, whose English name was Green, say he had killed enough white people for himself and pony to swim in their blood. We also heard him relate the first instance of his taking the life of a white person. It was when he was a boy, some fourteen years of age. A company of "braves" were going into a white settlement for the purpose of taking scalps and plunder. He obtained permission to accompany them on condition, or promise, that he would be brave. On arriving at the settlement, the first night, he and another young Indian were sent to reconnoiter a cabin. They returned and reported that there were no persons there except one man and one woman. They were ordered to go back and kill them. They returned to the cabin, and while this man and woman were sitting before the fire, perhaps not thinking of danger, they shot them through an opening in one of the jambs, entered the cabin, scalped them, and returned to their comrades with their bloody trophies. From this time forth, Green was a "brave" among the warriors.

The hardships endured by the settlers, and the dangers to which they were exposed tended to unite them together in ties of the strongest friendship. They were, indeed, a band of brothers and sisters ever ready to lend a helping hand to each other. If a stranger found his way to a settler's cabin, he was received with a cordial welcome and treated to the best the cabin possessed, and allowed to remain till it was his pleasure to depart.

The etiquette of these frontiersmen was not of the *city style*, but it was agreeable and easily observed. When you came to a cabin door, there being no *door-bell* to ring, your salutation would be: "Who keeps the house?" to which the rejoinder from within was: "Housekeepers! Come in." The cupboard-ware of the first settlers consisted principally of pewter and tin—pewter dishes, pewter bowls, pewter plates, pewter spoons, and tin buckets, tin coffee-pots, and tin cups. The good housewives of those days vied with each other in keeping the brightest pewter and tin, the brightest knives and forks, and the whitest puncheon floor.

With all the hardships and privations of those who went in the van of civilization, there were some sources of enjoyment not realized by those who came after them. They beheld the beauties of the forests in all their native grandeur, before they were marred by the hand of man. They inhaled the sweet odors from a thousand wild flowers which grew in nature's garden, as they were wafted upon the morning and evening air. They saw the numerous flocks and herds of buffalo and deer, God's "cattle upon a thousand hills," as they gazed upon virgin pasture fields of unsurpassed luxuriance, and they were charmed with the melody of the feathered songsters, as their heavenly strains were poured forth from the boughs of a thousand forest-trees. Then did the pious, far away in the wilderness, realize that

> " The birds of the air
> Sang anthems of praise
> While they went to prayer."

The union of hearts, the warm, true friendship existing among the first settlers in Indiana, was a source of the purest enjoyment to them. With all their rough backwoods habits, their lack of the means of mental culture, they exhibited in their lives the keeping of the great commandment, "Thou shalt love thy neighbor as thyself."

But these hardy, venturous, true, honest pioneers are nearly all gone. A few years more and the last one of their number will sleep silently in the grave. The few who still survive look with admiration upon the wonderful changes which have been wrought within the last sixty years. Sixty years more will doubtless produce greater changes.

CHAPTER III.

INTRODUCTION OF SCHOOLS.

ONE of the privations to which the first emigrants were subjected was the lack of schools. For a time none of any grade existed. When first introduced they were by no means of a high order, but the people were very glad to get them, such as they were. The school-houses were small log structures, capable of accommodating from fifteen to twenty-five scholars. A school of twenty-five was considered very large. Nearly the whole of one end of the school-house was cut out for the fireplace and chimney. A log in one end or side was removed for the purpose of affording light, along which a writing-desk was arranged by placing a broad board upon pins or supporters driven into the wall. The seats were made of hewn timbers with legs inserted in auger-holes. One of these benches was placed on either side of the fireplace, and a third in front, thus forming three sides of a square. One also was placed along side the writing-desk. These benches were made so high that the smaller children when seated could not reach the floor with their feet. This afforded the little fellows an opportunity of taking physical exercise while studying their lessons, they swinging their feet almost perpetually, and with as much precision as a regiment of soldiers keep the step when on parade or in the field drilling.

The rules for the government and general management of these schools differed to some extent. In some the rule was for the scholars to be at the school-house as early in the morning as possible, if that was by the time the sun was up. They were then kept till near the going down of the sun, even in the long Summer days. The employers went upon the principle that a school-teacher should work *all* day, like a man hired to work in the field. The scholars were considered to be under the control of the teacher from the time they left home in the morning till they returned in the evening, and were responsible to him for any misdemeanor going to or returning from school.

Fighting, quarreling, or the use of profane language were strictly forbidden. No recess or intermission was given, but one "play-spell" of from one hour to one and a half, at noon. But one scholar at a time was allowed to go out during school hours.

The punishment most generally inflicted for a breach of the rules was by the use of the rod or ferule, laid on in proportion to the offense. As an additional punishment the offender was sometimes sent into the grove to cut the rod with which he was to be punished. The boys were sometimes

INTRODUCTION OF SCHOOLS. 37

quite mischievous, and did not much regard a light flogging so they could have a little fun.

The play-time at noon was looked forward to by the scholars as a season of great enjoyment. The sports most delighted in were "bull-pen," "town-ball," "cat," "prison-base," and "fox-and hounds." The scholars were not arranged in classes for recitation, but each one recited by himself. In some schools, they recited, each day, in the order in which they arrived at the school-house in the morning. The one who arrived first, recited first, and so on. In this way the teacher kept himself constantly employed.

The New Testament was a common school-book. The school was opened in the morning by reading a chapter in the New Testament, all capable of reading standing up and reading his verse in regular consecutive order. In some schools, the scholars were taught to pronounce the letter *Z, Iz-zard;* in some, *Zed.* Those studying arithmetic were usually allowed to pursue their studies out of doors. In the Winter season, they would build a large fire to keep themselves warm.

It was difficult to procure school-teachers, and, when obtained, their qualifications were quite limited. One who could teach orthography, reading, writing, and arithmetic as far as the Single Rule of Three, was considered well qualified. In these schools, humble and unpretending as they were, some men who have arisen to eminence as physicians, lawyers, statesmen, and ministers of the Gospel, received their first instruction in letters.

Though the schools in Indiana were humble, and of a low grade at first, no State in the Union has made more rapid or greater advancement in educational facilities in the same length of time. She was organized as a Territory in 1800. Indiana University was incorporated in 1807, but did not go into operation for several years afterward. Now, she has seven universities and colleges for young men, three colleges for young women, a number of collegiate institutes and academies, with a system of free schools, in successful operation. The Hoosier State has been the subject of many slurs, in certain quarters, and much has been said about the number of persons that can neither read nor write; but if the facts were presented, they would show that nineteen-twentieths of that number are not natives of the State, nor were they brought into the State while they were children of proper age to go to school.

CHAPTER IV.

THE MORALS OF THE PEOPLE.

MANY of those who have never lived on the frontier, but who have been born and brought up in cities or the older portions of the country, are possibly disposed to think that frontiersmen must be a wicked, vulgar class of persons; but such is not the case. While some of those who first settled in Indiana were wicked persons, the great majority were moral, honest, virtuous, industrious men and women. Drunkenness, gambling, profanity, Sabbath desecration, and fighting, were the exceptions, not the common practice. The inhabitants of some neighborhoods were more loose in their morals than those of others. The first emigrants settled in squads or small colonies, forming neighborhoods. Miles of unbroken forest intervened between these settlements. In some of them wickedness was more prevalent than in others. In some it was a rare thing to hear an oath uttered, or the report of a hunter's gun on the holy Sabbath day, or to see a man drunk. To do any of these things was deemed disgraceful. The general sentiment was against all these vices. For several years after the eastern portion of Indiana began to be settled such a thing as the murder of one white man by another was not known.

The first murder in all the eastern portion of the State, from the Ohio River to Fort Wayne, occurred in Wayne county. A man by the name of Criss killed his son-in-law, Chambers. It was induced by Chambers's wife. She made complaint, from time to time, to Criss, her father, of bad treatment by her husband. Criss went to the house of Chambers and attacked him with a butcher-knife. Chambers started to run. Criss seized a gun which hung over the door and shot him as he ran. He fell and expired, without speaking, in a few moments. Mrs. Flint, who lived in the neighborhood, was present and witnessed the whole transaction. This murder created great excitement throughout the whole country. Criss was arrested and thrown into prison in Salisbury. The jail was a log building having two rooms. When the Circuit Court came on he was brought to trial. The principal witnesses against him were his wife and daughter (Mrs. Chambers), a son, and Mrs. Flint. He was found guilty, and condemned to be hung. The day of his execution was a memorable day to the people. The fact that a *man was to be hung* seemed to strike every one with awe. Even the children were so impressed with the thought that a *man* was to be *hung* that day they spoke almost in whispers. When the day of execution arrived the people gathered by scores and hundreds at the

THE MORALS OF THE PEOPLE. 41

county seat from many miles around to witness the solemn scene.

At the appointed hour the criminal was taken from the jail, where he had been chained down to the floor from the time he was condemned, and conveyed to the gallows in a wagon, seated upon his coffin, guarded by a company of armed men. At the gallows Rev. Daniel Fraly, a Methodist minister, stood in the wagon and preached a very impressive sermon to the people. Criss sat upon his coffin during the delivery of the sermon, and looked upon the audience without showing any signs of excitement. At the close of the sermon the rope was adjusted around his neck, the cap drawn over his face, and the wagon was driven from under him. After a few minutes of hard struggling all was over. The blood-stained soul passed into the presence of a just God. Criss exhibited no signs of penitence during his confinement nor under the gallows. This was the first execution in all that region of the country, and occurred in the Spring of 1816.

Far removed from the vices of the crowded city or the more populous portions of the old States, shut up in the wilderness, dependent upon their industry for a support, the first settlers had no time to spend in idleness or pleasure-seeking. Every man and woman labored with their hands. Their time and attention being honestly employed, the prolific sources of crime were cut off. And yet the people were not *all* pious. With all the improvements in the State in the arts and sciences, agriculture and internal improvements, it is doubtful whether the morals of the people, in proportion to population, are so good as they were fifty years ago. All the vices practiced by the people then are practiced now, together with many others. If it be true that morality and religion have not kept pace with the increase of population and the general improvement in the State, it is much to be lamented. The examination of the subject is worthy the attention of the Churches.

CHAPTER V.

THE INTRODUCTION OF THE GOSPEL AMONG THE FIRST SETTLERS.

MANY of those who first settled the Territory of Indiana were members of Churches before they emigrated. Some were Methodists, some Baptists, some Presbyterians, some Quakers. Much the largest portion were Methodists and Baptists. Coming from the older portions of the country, where they enjoyed church privileges—where they often heard the Gospel preached—they keenly felt the loss now that they were inhabitants of the wilderness. Though no sound of the church-going bell was heard on the holy Sabbath to call them to devotion, and though there were no ministers of the Lord Jesus to unfold to them the promises of God, or tell the sweet story of the Cross or of the joys of heaven, and administer to them the holy sacraments, yet they did not lay aside their Christian professions. They set up the family altar in their newly-erected cabins, on which they regularly offered their morning and evening sacrifices.

When one of them visited a neighbor to spend a social evening, among other topics of conversation, religion, and the many happy hours they had enjoyed in the sanctuary in other days and years, formed a prominent part, and they always closed the evening's sociability with prayer. When the Sabbath returned, they gathered together and held a prayer meeting, or some one read a sermon from some volume he had brought with him from beyond the mountains.

These pioneer Christians felt that, as sin was always offensive to God, grievous to the Holy Spirit, and had caused the Savior to bleed and die, so also it should be grievous to them. They never allowed any one to sin in their presence without reproof. This was so well known among those who were disposed to be irreligious that they seldom allowed themselves to sin in the presence of these Christians in the wilderness.

These pious men and women, though without a shepherd to be their spiritual guide, were, indeed, "the salt of the earth." They looked with anxious eyes and longing hearts for the coming of the heralds of the Cross. They constantly prayed that the Great Head of the Church would send his messengers among them. When they did make their appearance, they were hailed with delight, and welcomed as ministering angels, sent of God to comfort and strengthen them in the faith of the Gospel. When, in their wilderness habitations, they first heard the "joyful sound," it was, to them, "good news from a far country." On it their souls fed and feasted. The heaven-originated Methodist

INTRODUCTION OF THE GOSPEL. 45

itinerant system brought the first shepherds to these sheep in the wilderness.

Though the Methodist itinerant system has been violently opposed and ridiculed, it was *that* which first brought the Gospel into Indiana. Though the itinerant Methodist preachers have been stigmatized as "itinerant circuit-riders," THEY were the men who first threaded the Indian-traces and the newly-blazed ways in search of the lost sheep of the House of Israel. They were the men who swam rivers, slept in the woods alone at night, among wild beasts and savage men, in order to carry the glad tidings of salvation to the first settlers.

Indiana is more indebted to *itinerant Methodist preachers* for the high position she now occupies in science, literature, and Christianity, than to any other class of men. Though these ministers of the Lord Jesus were not cultured men, as that term is ordinarily understood, they were, nevertheless, educated in an exalted sense. Their education was such as to qualify them for their peculiar and important work. They were inured to hardship; they knew how to sympathize with those to whom they ministered; they could readily accommodate themselves to the circumstances by which they were surrounded, and could always make themselves agreeable in the loneliest cabin. They all had a *fair*, some of them a *good*, English training. Some of them, while traveling their large circuits, pursued their studies till they became good Latin, Greek, and Hebrew scholars. They were well read in the Holy Scriptures, and when they preached they *used* them. It would have been an anomaly to have heard one of these men preach a sermon and never make a quotation from the Scriptures, except when he read his text.

These men were fearless in the discharge of duty, counting not their lives dear if they might win souls to Christ. No privation, no hardship, no danger deterred them. They were bold in their attacks upon Satan's kingdom, which, by the power of the Holy Spirit that attended their preaching, was often made to rock from center to circumference. No sin, great or small, in high or low places, was allowed to go unscathed. Fear of offending, even the most influential, formed no part of their programme. Their eyes were singly fixed upon the glory of God in the salvation of souls.

It frequently occurred, when these self-sacrificing men of God were making their bold charges upon the ranks of Satan, in the name of the Great Captain of their salvation, that those who were marshaled under hell's dark banner would call for quarter, and, falling upon their knees, commence pleading for mercy. On one occasion, at a camp meeting, while one of these ministers, who was a real "son of thunder," was pouring out the terrors of the law, describing the torments of the damned in such awful horror that it seemed their dreadful groans could almost be heard, and while the thunders from Sinai's smoking top rolled long and loud, an old Revolutionary soldier who was standing in the rear of the congregation, came rushing toward the preachers' stand, crying at the top of his voice: "Quarter! quarter! quarter!" and falling upon his knees, said: "I am an old soldier; I have fought through the Revolutionary War; I have heard the cannon's loud roar, and have seen blood and brains flying in every direction around me; but since God made me, I never heard such cannonading as this. I yield! I yield!"

Some of these ministers, who first planted the Gospel standard, were truly eloquent, and would hold the listening crowds that attended their preaching spell-bound, swaying them like forest trees before the mighty blast.

While those holy men led the van, they were supported by as noble, brave, and true a band of Christian men and women as ever fought under the blood-stained banner of Prince Immanuel. "They shunned no cross; despised no shame." Some of them were mighty in prayer and exhortation.

The women of those days were gifted in prayer, and often prayed in the public congregation. We have heard them, while they took hold of the horns of God's altar by faith, and pleaded with an earnestness and power that seemed to bring heaven and earth together. These ministers and members are nearly all gone. They have crossed the river, grounded their arms at Jesus' feet, and have been crowned "heirs of eternal life." But they are worthy "to be had in everlasting remembrance." When *they* fell in the ranks of God's sacramental host, ending their warfare with the shout of triumph, there were no religious periodicals in which to publish to the Church and the world an account of their holy lives and triumphant deaths. We shall give a more extended notice of some of them hereafter.

CHAPTER VI.

INTRODUCTION OF METHODISM.

It has generally been thought that Methodism was introduced into Indiana in what is known as Clark's Grant, which included a great portion of what is now Clark and Floyd counties. In later years it has been stated that a class of Methodists was formed in Clark's Grant as early as 1802; but upon what evidence or authority we do not know. We do know that Rev. Hugh Cull, a local preacher, settled in the Whitewater country as early as 1805, having visited the country the year previous.

The first circuit in Indiana was called Whitewater, and belonged to the Ohio district, in the old Western Conference. It embraced all the country from the Ohio River along the eastern line of the Territory as far north as there were any white settlements, which was in the region where Richmond now stands, and west to the land belonging to the Indians. This circuit was probably formed in 1807. It appears upon the Minutes of the Western Conference in the year 1808, with Joseph Williams as preacher in charge, and John Sale presiding elder of the district.

The settlements visited by Mr. Williams were

remote from each other. The traveling was laborious and hazardous. The roads along which he had to pass were Indian traces and newly-blazed ways. The streams were unbridged; the country was full of ravenous beasts and of the much-dreaded Indians. The emigrants to whom he ministered could afford him but few accommodations. He labored faithfully hunting up the Methodists who had pitched their tents in the wilderness, and at the end of the year returned one hundred and sixty-five white members and one colored.

According to the most reliable data, these were all the Methodists who had, to this date, been organized and numbered in Indiana. In 1808 Indiana contained but one circuit, with 166 members of the Methodist Episcopal Church. Now, 1866, there are four Annual Conferences, with a membership of about 100,000 in the State. How great the change in fifty-eight years! Mr. Williams has the honor of being the first itinerant Methodist preacher appointed to a circuit in Indiana. We would, if we had the particulars of his life and death, give them to the public to perpetuate his memory. In 1809 he was sent to Scioto circuit, in the State of Ohio, and in 1810 he located.

In 1809 Indiana district was formed, and Samuel Parker was appointed presiding elder. It was composed of the following circuits: Illinois, Missouri, Maramack, Coldwater, Whitewater, and Silver Creek. Though but two circuits of this district were

INTRODUCTION OF METHODISM.   51

in Indiana, we give its entire bounds, that the young men who are now traveling circuits and districts in the State may see the extent of the fields of labor our fathers had to cultivate. This district covered all the Territories of Indiana, Illinois, and Missouri. It required surely a man of strong nerves and stout heart to travel such a district at such a time. In traveling this district Mr. Parker had to go from the eastern boundary of Indiana across Illinois, and then across the Mississippi River into Missouri. In some places many miles of unbroken wilderness intervened between the settlements he had to visit. This year Silver Creek circuit was formed, and embraced all the settlements in the southern portion of the Territory, and up the Ohio River to Whitewater circuit. Hector Sanford and Moses Crume were appointed to Whitewater, and Josiah Crawford to Silver Creek. The most northern appointment on the Whitewater circuit was the cabin of George Smith, which was about two miles from where the city of Richmond is now situated.

At the close of this year the preachers returned 352 members for Whitewater circuit, and 188 for Silver Creek, making an increase of 374. In 1810 Whitewater was placed in the Miami district, with John Sale presiding elder, and Thomas Nelson and Samuel H. Thompson circuit preachers. This district was composed of the following circuits: Cincinnati, Mad River, Scioto, Deer Creek, Hockhocking, White Oak, and Whitewater.

Silver Creek was in the Green River district, William Burke presiding elder, and Sela Pain circuit preacher. This district was composed of the following circuits: Green River, Barren, Wayne, Cumberland, Danville, Salt River, Shelby, and Silver Creek. Indiana district was composed of Illinois, Missouri, Maramack, Coldwater, Cape Girardeau, and Vincennes circuits. Samuel Parker was returned to the district, and William Winans was appointed to Vincennes. Nelson and Thompson, who traveled the Whitewater circuit this year, both rose to considerable distinction, particularly Mr. Thompson. The next year Nelson was sent to Rapids circuit, in Mississippi. Mr. Thompson was sent to Nollichuckie, in the State of Tennessee. Neither of these men ever returned to Indiana to labor.

Sela Pain, who traveled the Silver Creek circuit this year, was sent the next to Natchez circuit, Mississippi.

Vincennes circuit appears on the Minutes of the Conference this year for the first time, making three fields of labor in Indiana. What the dimensions of this circuit were, at its formation, we have no means of knowing. Vincennes was an old French post, under the influence of the Roman Catholics; a hard place in which to plant Methodism. Mr. Winans, who had been sent to Vincennes this year, had been admitted on trial in the Western Conference the year before. He was a young man of promising talents, and made a good impression on those who heard him preach. It was difficult for him to get the people of Vincennes to come to preaching, so wicked and so much were they under the influence of the Romish priests.

The following incident is said to have occurred this year: General William H. Harrison was Governor of the Territory of Indiana, and resided at Vincennes. Young Mr. Winans had an appointment to preach one night, in a small room in town. General Harrison and one other person composed the congregation assembled to hear the young preacher. There was but one candle to give light, and nothing to place *that* upon. The General held the candle for the young preacher to see to read his hymn and text. Mr. Winans preached faithfully to those two hearers. After this he had no trouble in getting a congregation to preach to.

From Vincennes Mr. Winans was sent to Attakapas circuit, in the Mississippi district, Louisiana. This was the only year he labored in Indiana. He rose to considerable distinction; received the degree of D. D., and was several times elected to General Conference. He was a member of the General Conference of 1844, which met in the city of New York, and took an active part in the great discussion on the subject of slavery. He was one of the prominent leaders in the formation of the Methodist Episcopal Church South. He died a few years since. Some of his family still reside in the South, and were violently opposed to the United States Government during the late rebellion.

At the close of this year the preachers returned 484 members from Whitewater circuit, 235 from Silver Creek, and 43 from Vincennes, making a total of 765, an increase of 418, showing that Methodism began to take a deep hold upon the pioneers in Indiana.

In 1811 Whitewater circuit was continued in connection with the Miami district, Solomon Langdon presiding elder, and Moses Crume in charge of the circuit. The people hailed Mr. Crume's return to them with great delight. He had traveled the circuit as junior preacher two years before. He made his impress upon the people so deeply this year that he was ever afterward a great favorite among them.

Isaac Lindsey was sent to Silver Creek circuit this year. It remained in connection with the Green River district, with William Burke as presiding elder.

Vincennes appears on the Minutes this year as "St. Vincennes," in connection with the Cumberland district, Learner Blackman presiding elder, and Thomas Stilwell circuit preacher. Mr. Blackman was a man eminent for his talents, piety, and usefulness. During the course of his life he traveled over a very extensive territory of country, ranging from Pittsburg to New Orleans, and was highly esteemed by all who knew him. This year

INTRODUCTION OF METHODISM. 55

the preachers reported 368 members from Whitewater circuit, 397 from Silver Creek, and 325 from Vincennes, making a total of 1,160, or an increase of 395.

In 1812 two additional circuits were formed in Indiana—Lawrenceburg and Patoka. Whitewater and Lawrenceburg were connected with the Miami district, Solomon Langdon presiding elder. Silver Creek was connected with Salt River district, James Ware presiding elder, while Vincennes and Patoka were connected with Wabash district, James Axley presiding elder. Walter Griffith was sent to Lawrenceburg, Robert W. Finley to Whitewater, William M'Mehan to Silver Creek, James Turner to Vincennes, and Benjamin Edge to Patoka. These men were all faithful and useful. Some of them were men of note. Rev. Jacob Young, in his "Autobiography," and Bishop Morris, in his Miscellany, speak in high terms of James Axley, the presiding elder this year of Wabash district. He was a man of a peculiar order of talents, and very noted for his eccentricities. Many amusing and interesting anecdotes are related of him. Bishop Morris somewhere relates the following as his introduction to Mr. Axley, while the Bishop was attending the Holston Conference, soon after he had been elected and ordained to the Episcopal office. As he was walking along the street in the town where the Conference was in session, he suddenly felt himself in the grasp of some one who had come up from behind him. The stranger holding him fast said, "This is Bishop Morris, I suppose?" The Bishop answered, "It is what is left of him." "Well," said the stranger, as he eyed him from head to feet, "I think the General Conference was scarce of Bishop timber when they made a *Bishop* out of *you.*"

Walter Griffith, who traveled the Lawrenceburg circuit this year, was afterward made presiding elder, and filled that important office with great acceptability and usefulness. Robert W. Finley had been a Presbyterian minister for several years, and was the father of Rev. James B. Finley, who rose to such distinction in Ohio. At the close of this year there were returned from the five circuits in Indiana a total membership of 1,121, which seems to present a decrease in the number of Church members; but from some cause there were no returns from Lawrenceburg and Patoka circuits. This accounts for the apparent decrease in the number of members.

In 1813 the old Western Conference was divided or discontinued, and the Ohio and Tennessee Conferences were formed out of it. The circuits in Indiana were placed in these two Conferences. Lawrenceburg and Whitewater were placed in the Miami district, and Silver Creek in the Salt River district, all within the boundary lines of Ohio Conference. Patoka disappears this year. William Dixon was sent to Lawrenceburg, John Strange

INTRODUCTION OF METHODISM. 57

went to Whitewater, and Thomas Nelson to Silver Creek.

Vincennes was placed in the Wabash district, Tennessee Conference, with Peter Cartwright presiding elder, and Richard Richards circuit preacher. This being the year when the war with Great Britain and her Indian allies was in full blast, the exposures and privations of the itinerant Methodist preachers were greatly increased. The dangers from the Indians, the deadly enemy of the whites, now encouraged and strengthened by the British, were so great that the settlers most generally gathered into forts which they had erected for their safety, In order that they might preach to them, the preachers had to follow the settlers to these forts. Indeed, they had few or no preaching-places except forts. Some of these self-sacrificing men of God, for their own safety, carried their guns with them whenever traveling from fort to fort to preach to their flocks. This state of things deranged the plans of the circuits and the classes very much; but it did not destroy the religious fervor of these pious Methodists, shut up in their stockades. When one of these itinerants, with his gun on his shoulder, called at the gates of one of these forts, it was immediately swung open by the inmates, and he received in as the Lord's messenger; and while preaching the Word of Life to them, the holy fire which burned in their hearts would be raised to such a flame that the shout of "a King in the camp" was heard. These were glorious "times of refreshing from the presence of the Lord." The writer, though then a small boy, remembers well some of those seasons in the fort at his father's.

At the close of this year the number of Church members reported was as follows:

Lawrenceburg	489
Whitewater	847
Silver Creek	555
Vincennes	175
Patoka	110
Total membership	2,176

In five years, two thousand, one hundred and seventy-six members had been gathered into the Methodist Episcopal Church in Indiana, and this though the country was new and though but a small portion of the Territory was inhabited by white people.

This large increase shows that the men who had been sent into the wild wilderness to cultivate Immanuel's land had done their work faithfully, and God had crowned their labors with success.

In 1814 Moses Crume was sent to Lawrenceburg circuit, David Sharp to Whitewater, Charles Harrison to Silver Creek, and Zachariah Witten to Vincennes. Patoka does not appear in the list of appointments for this year. Charles Holliday was appointed presiding elder of Salt River district, and Silver Creek being in his district gave him connection with the work in Indiana; and Jesse

INTRODUCTION OF METHODISM. 59

Walker being presiding elder of Illinois district, and Vincennes being in that district, he was brought in connection with the work in Indiana. The number of members reported at the close of this year was 1,759, showing a decrease, which was caused by the derangement of the work produced by the war in which the country was then engaged. In 1815 John Strange was sent to Lawrenceburg, William Hunt to Whitewater, Shadrach Ruark to Silver Creek, John Scripps to Patoka, and John Shrader to Vincennes, with the same presiding elders that traveled the districts the year before. The number of circuits was not increased, but their boundaries were greatly enlarged.

The terror among the settlers, caused by the war, and the constant danger from the Indians that infested the country by thousands, had caused many of the inhabitants to return to the old States for safety. Among them were many Methodists, causing a large decrease this year. There were reported to Conference a total of 1,504.

In 1816 David Sharp was sent to Lawrenceburg, Daniel Fraly to Whitewater, Joseph Kinkade to Silver Creek, John Shrader to Blue River, Thomas A. King to Patoka, and Thomas Davis to Vincennes. Blue River circuit had been formed out of a part of Silver Creek. It extended down the Ohio River, and out to the head-waters of Patoka. We now have six circuits formed in Indiana. The war being over, and the country becoming more quiet, the inhabitants who had fled for fear of the Indians began to return, with many new emigrants. The preachers were enabled to report this year a total of 1,877 members, an increase of 373 over the past year.

In 1817 Russel Bigelow was sent to Lawrenceburg, Benjamin Lawrence to Whitewater, Daniel M'Henry and Thomas Davis to Patoka, James M'Cord and Charles Slocumb to Vincennes, John Cord to Blue River, and Joseph Pownel to Silver Creek.

Missouri Conference having been formed, all of Illinois, and all of Indiana, except Lawrenceburg and Whitewater circuits, were placed in that Conference. The other circuits were in the Illinois district, with Samuel H. Thompson for presiding elder. Moses Crume was placed on the Miami district, in the Ohio Conference, which brought him back to Lawrenceburg and Whitewater circuits, where he met a hearty welcome from the people. The preachers on the six circuits in Indiana reported at the close of this year a total membership of 1,907, being a small increase over the past year.

In 1818 Samuel West and Allen Wiley were sent to Lawrenceburg, William Hunt to Whitewater, Charles Slocumb to Patoka, Thomas Davis to Little Pigeon, John Shrader and John M'Cord to Vincennes, Othniel Talbert to Blue River, and John Cord to Silver Creek. Little Pigeon was a new circuit just formed, and embraced the country

INTRODUCTION OF METHODISM. 61

south-west of Blue River circuit. We have now seven circuits, traveled by nine preachers. The preachers reported to Conference at the close of this year a total of 3,044 members, an increase of 1,037.

We have now given a brief sketch of the introduction and progress of Methodism in Indiana, so far as the formation of districts and circuits, and the men appointed to travel them, is concerned, for the first decade. We will now turn our attention to some other particulars connected with the introduction of Methodism into the State.

CHAPTER VII.

MEETING-HOUSES.

The first places of public worship were the cabins of the emigrants. Some of these were large enough to hold from fifty to one hundred persons. A congregation of one hundred persons was considered large in those days. During the Summer and Autumn, the people frequently resorted to the grove for public worship. A rough stand was erected, and seats made of split logs, properly arranged. At these stands circuit preaching through all the warm season was had; also Sabbath prayer meetings, and sometimes two days' meetings were conducted at them. Often the power of the Holy One came down among the people, and nature's temple was made to ring with high halleluias. These Christians felt that in God's own temple they could speak forth the praises of the Most High, and pour out the joy and gratitude of their hearts without restraint.

As soon as it was possible, having first to erect their cabins, clear a little ground, and prepare to raise bread for their families, they commenced the work of building houses for the Lord. Saw-mills were few and far between, and the only carpenter's tools the country afforded were axes, hand-saws, drawing-knives, and augers; consequently, the meeting-houses were of rough construction. They were of logs, covered with clap-boards, held on by weight-poles. The floors were of puncheons; the chimneys of sticks and clay, and the seats of split logs, hewn smoothly with an ax. The pulpits were of clap-boards, shaved nicely with a drawing-knife. A window was cut out immediately in the rear of the pulpit, to give light for the preacher to see to read his hymns, Scripture-lessons, and text. In some cases this was the only window in the house. Such meeting-houses were the best the people could afford. They erected them with much earnest prayer. When they were ready for use, they were, in the most solemn manner, offered to the Great Head of the Church, as a place for him to dwell in; a place where they might "worship him in spirit and in truth." In these rudely-constructed temples of the Most High the Gospel was preached in its purity. Saints and sinners "received their portion in due season." There was no compromising with sin, no studying to please the worldly-minded, nor disposition to avoid giving offense to the half-hearted, formal professors of religion. The law was fulminated from Sinai's blazing top. Hell, with its sulphurous flames and the groans of the damned, were portrayed in words that burned. The love of God to man in the gift of his Son; the humiliation and condescension of the Savior in coming into the world to suffer, bleed, and die; his poverty and sorrow;

his agony in the garden; his betrayal; his crucifixion on the cross; his last cry—"It is finished;" his resurrection from the tomb, and his ascension, were each and all presented to the people in colors of living light that won the heart and caused tears of joy to flow like showers of rain. Worship among the first settlers was real, spiritual, soul-worship. They had not the temptations to pride and self-gratulation when at the place of worship which may beset those who pay their devotions in splendid church edifices, sitting on cushioned seats, and kneeling—if they kneel at all—on Brussels carpets.

We are not entering a *protest* against fine churches. Of all houses God's house should be *most* magnificent. It is questionable, however, whether the spending of seventy-five or one hundred or one hundred and fifty thousand dollars to build a church for one congregation to worship in, when there are so many places where God's poor have *no* house of worship, and when so much of the world is still in heathen and pagan darkness, is pleasing to the Divine Being. It requires much watching, much close self-examination, and constant prayer, to avoid becoming vain of our fine churches. The tendency is strong to forget Christ's poor; and we fear that sometimes we push aside the statement that Christ himself was so poor when on earth that he cried, "The foxes have holes, and the birds of the air have nests, but the Son of Man hath not where to lay his head."

MEETING-HOUSES. 65

One of the first, if not *the* first, Methodist meeting-houses built in Indiana was erected in what is now Wayne county, in 1808. In this year the first circuit was formed. It was called "Whitewater." This meeting-house was at the time the upper or most northern appointment on that circuit. There being no circuit formed in any other part of the Territory prior to 1808, it may be presumed there were no meeting-houses built at an earlier date. The one referred to was called "Meek's Meeting-House," and was built on Clear creek, a little to the southeast and about one mile and a half from where Salisbury, the first county seat of Wayne county, was afterward located. This house was occupied as a preaching-place for several years. After Salisbury was laid out and began to improve, preaching was moved to the town, and the old log meeting-house was abandoned. To this meeting-house the writer was carried by his parents when an infant, and there dedicated to God in holy baptism by the Rev. Moses Crume, who was then traveling Whitewater circuit. So far as we know, there is not a member of the Church who worshiped in this meeting-house now living, and but *one* surviving of all the ministers who preached in that house, and he is far advanced in life. If all are safely housed in heaven, how great the contrast! Once they worshiped together in this world in a log temple, surrounded by wild beasts and savage men. Now they worship together in heaven, in a "house not made with hands," surrounded by angels, the prophets, and apostles. O, happy saints! wait and watch! We, your descendants, who still sorrow below, are following on.

The second Methodist meeting-house erected in Wayne county was built on land belonging to John Cain, about three miles north-west of where Richmond now stands. It was called "Cain's Meeting-House." It was a log structure, about eighteen by twenty-two feet, the chimney in one end. When it was ready for occupancy, a day for its presentation to the Great Head of the Church was appointed. When the time for the solemn services arrived, the people—men, women, and children—gathered in from the surrounding neighborhood. The dedication sermon was preached by John Summerville, who was then traveling the Oxford circuit in the State of Ohio. His text was Zechariah x, 4: "Out of him came forth the corner, out of him the nail, out of him the battle-bow, out of him every oppressor together." A singular text for a dedication sermon.

In this small log-house some of the most talented men of the West have preached the unsearchable riches of Christ; among the number Moses Crume, John Strange, Walter Griffith, Alexander Cummins, Augustus Jocelyn, James Jones, Arthur W. Elliott, Russel Bigelow, Allen Wiley, and James Havens. One sermon preached in the house by Augustus Jocelyn, from 2 Peter ii, 22—"But it has happened

MEETING-HOUSES. 67

unto them according to the true proverb; the dog is returned to his own vomit again, and the sow that was washed to her wallowing in the mire"— made an impression on the minds of some who heard it that time can never erase. O, the dreadful state of the backslider as portrayed by the preacher that day!

These distinguished men of God have all passed away. Their voices are no more heard among men, but "their works do follow them."

Cain's meeting-house has long since disappeared, and perhaps but few, if any, who now reside in that neighborhood know that there ever was such a place of worship.

The third meeting-house erected in Wayne county was called "Salem," and was built where the town of Boston now stands. It was of larger dimensions and made a finer appearance than either of the others. This house was occupied as a place of worship for a number of years. In it the power of God was displayed in a wonderful manner. Many souls were enlisted in the army of the Lord, and many here first tasted the joys of pardoned sin. A large society was built up, and the town of Boston, where the old Salem Church once stood, is now the head of a circuit in the South-Eastern Indiana Conference.

The first frame meeting-house built in Wayne county by the Methodists was erected under the administration of Rev. James Havens, in the town of Centerville. The members of the Church, in the bounds of the circuit, were generally poor. Mr. Havens carried a subscription paper with him as he passed round the circuit, and solicited aid to build as opportunity offered. He presented his subscription paper to Elisha W. Fulton, an excellent man and class-leader who then lived in Richmond. Mr. Fulton was not opulent. His occupation was making Windsor chairs. Times were hard and money scarce. He could exchange his chairs for produce, but seldom could sell them for cash. He greatly desired to aid in the erection of the church, but felt his embarrassment. He finally offered Mr. Havens a set of ten-dollar chairs. Mr. Havens said, "No, subscribe *five* dollars and the Lord will send some man to buy your chairs, and you will *save* five dollars." Mr. Fulton thought a moment. He determined to trust the Lord. He subscribed five dollars, and Mr. Havens went on his way rejoicing. The next day a gentleman from Centerville came over to Richmond, bought a set of chairs of Mr. Fulton, and paid him ten dollars in cash. Mr. Fulton laid by five dollars for Mr. Havens, and when he came round again paid the sum and had his *five* left. No one ever loses any thing by trusting the Divine Being. By subscriptions of ten, five, and one dollar, the necessary funds to build the meeting-house were procured. Israel Abrams gave fifty dollars, which was then considered and was really a large amount to be given by

MEETING-HOUSES. 69

one man. It would be pleasant to give accounts of the erection of the first meeting-houses in other parts of Indiana had we the data. No doubt many interesting incidents connected with their history might be given, but unless some other pen writes them out they will never be furnished to the public.

Since the first rude log meeting-house was erected in Indiana, the work of church-building has gone on, till in almost every village and neighborhood a Methodist church may be seen. In some of our cities there are as many as five or six. At this time the number of Methodist churches in the State reaches to some thirteen hundred. Some of them are of the finest architecture, costing from thirty to seventy thousand dollars.

The advancement in this department of Christian enterprise in Indiana, for the last fifty years, has been equal to that of any other State in the Union, in proportion to population. Those who assemble in their richly-furnished churches can not fully sympathize with those who worshiped in their small log meeting-houses, in the wilderness. The worship in our elegant churches is, perhaps, more formal than it was when our fathers and mothers paid their homage to Jehovah in the simply-constructed temples of their own hands, or under the shade of the closely-interlocked forest trees. Our congregations now present a much more gay appearance than then; nevertheless, God has still true worshipers. And, though in some of our churches there are instruments to assist in "making melody unto the Lord," there is the power of the Holy One in them, and Christians are still "glad when it is said unto them, let us go up to the house of the Lord." They say, "Our feet shall stand within thy gates, O Jerusalem!"

CHAPTER VIII.

CAMP MEETINGS.

CAMP MEETINGS were highly prized by the Methodists of Indiana, in the first settling of the country. They were looked to with great anxiety from year to year. At the close of one camp meeting, the people looked forward to the next, as the period, when they should meet again in their annual convocation, and enjoy a rich "feast of tabernacles." At the conclusion of one, they made certain calculations on attending the next, if life and health were spared. They made it a rule to attend at least one camp meeting each year. If they were held in the midst of "crop time," or harvest, that did not prevent them from being present. They attended these gatherings in the woods, not for show, not to make a display, nor for pastime; but to enjoy communion with God, to get their spiritual strength renewed, to make war on Satan's legions, and to advance Christ's kingdom in the world. Sometimes the sons of Belial caused them a little trouble, but this did not discourage or cast down. Having laid aside the business cares of life, and left their homes, with all their earthly goods, in the keeping of Him whose eye neither slumbers nor sleeps, and going up in the strength of Israel's God, they felt that no weapon formed against them could prosper.

The time at these camp meetings was all devoted to worship, except what was absolutely necessary for eating and sleeping. None was devoted to idle or worldly conversation, in the tents or around the encampment. Not unfrequently when the battle commenced, it was continued day and night, without intermission. While some slept, others kept up the engagement, pouring hot shot into Satan's ranks. This continuous fire was such, that often the stoutest sinners, when once brought within its range, were made to yield and cry for quarter, in a very short space of time. Sometimes, at the midnight hour, the Gospel battery would open anew from the stand, while the infantry, at various points of the encampment, were charging the gates of hell by way of prayer meetings.

In such engagements the slain of the Lord were many. In several instances where the battle continued through the night; as the day dawned, victory, great and glorious, turned on Israel's side. As the light of the rising sun dispelled the darkness of the night, the Sun of Righteousness dispelled the moral darkness from many souls, and enabled them to see their names inscribed in heaven.

These camp meetings were the means of gathering many recruits for the army of the Lord. The membership of the Church was greatly strengthened thereby. "Camp-meeting-religion," as it has been sometimes sneeringly called, even by some who profess to be Christians, has stood the test of the severest trials. True, some who have been converted at them have fallen back; but a very large majority have stood firm, and proved steadfast. Thousands have gained the hights of immortality, and now sit down with Abraham, Isaac, and Jacob, in the kingdom above, to go out no more. Some of the brightest lights that have ever shone in the Church, ministers and laymen, were awakened and converted at camp meetings.

The closing exercises of these "feasts of tabernacles," were always most solemn and affecting. A procession of the members of the Church, headed by all the ministers present, with all serious persons falling in, marched around the encampment a few times, singing appropriate songs; the full chorus of every voice rose and swelled, while ever and anon loud halleluias would roll up from hearts too full to refrain any longer. A prayer was then offered, all in the procession kneeling. At its close the preachers took a position, when the procession moving on, all shook hands with them, bidding them farewell. With many, this was a *last* farewell. The eyes that did not weep on these occasions, at witnessing such a scene, were incapable of tears.

All having bidden the preachers farewell, the benediction was pronounced, when these children of the Most High separated, some of them to meet no more till called from labor to reward, the people returning to their homes, and the ministers to their distant fields of labor.

A camp meeting was held in what was then Dearborn, now Wayne county, about a mile south-east of where Salisbury was afterward laid out, in August or September, 1810. This was perhaps the first camp meeting held in Indiana. The country being new, and the inhabitants few, the number of persons in attendance was not large, but it was a time of power and great glory. A goodly number of the unconverted who attended this meeting were, before its close, happily brought to a knowledge of sins forgiven. The conversions were clear and satisfactory. Thomas Nelson and Samuel H. Thompson were the preachers on the circuit, and John Sale was the presiding elder. So far as we know, not a man or woman who attended this camp meeting is now living. Time's rolling stream has borne them all away.

From this place the camp meetings were moved farther east, to the land belonging to Rev. Hugh Cull, where they were continued for several years.

We would like to trace the history of camp meetings in Indiana had we the means of so doing. As the country improved and the number of circuits increased, almost every part of the State has witnessed the success of these instrumentalities for the accomplishment of good. No instrumentalities have ever been used by the Church which accomplished so much good in the same length of time and at the same cost. The advancement of the country in age, wealth, refinement, and the increase of the number of churches are not sufficient reasons to justify the laying them aside. At a camp meeting persons are kept under a religious influence as they can not be in a meeting held in a church in town or country. Often persons are awakened while at church, but go out and again mix with the unholy throng in the town or city and shake off their convictions, when, if they had been at a camp meeting and remained within the religious atmosphere there they would have yielded their stubborn hearts, sought and found mercy.

The Church is losing much by abandoning this means of grace, which has been so successful in the salvation of precious souls. When the country was new Methodists esteemed it a light matter to take their families in a wagon and travel twenty or thirty miles to a camp meeting. Now the facilities for traveling are such that the people, with but little labor, could travel forty or fifty miles with much less fatigue. As a general thing, to spend a week in the grove at a camp meeting in a pleasant season of the year, is conducive to physical health. Certainly no Christian can spend a few days at a properly-conducted camp meeting without being spiritually revived and strengthened.

CHAPTER IX.

FURTHER SKETCHES AND INCIDENTS OF THE EARLY SETTLEMENT OF INDIANA.

The first settlers were brave, fearless men and women, true to each other. The privations to which they were subjected, and the dangers with which they were surrounded, served as so many bonds in uniting them as a band of brothers and sisters.

When the war of "'12" and "'13," as it has been called, came on, the people of each settlement erected a fort at the cabin of some one of them, into which they gathered for safety. These forts, or stockades, were made of two rows of split timbers, some twelve or fourteen feet long, planted firmly in the ground, inclosing more or less ground, as the necessity demanded. There were large gates, made of hewn timbers of from three to six inches in thickness. Small cabins were erected inside the stockades for the accommodation of the families. Usually one block-house was built in each fort. These block-houses were two stories high, the upper story projecting over the lower, say two feet, with port-holes in the floor of the projection, so that the men could see to shoot the Indians if they succeeded in getting to the walls of the block-house.

There were likewise port-holes in the wall in the upper and lower stories, through which shooting of much execution could be performed as the foe was advancing.

Though five, ten, or more families, composed of children, from young men and women down to nursing babes, occupied these block-houses, it was a rare occurrence for any serious difficulty to arise among them. Sometimes provisions were scarce, but usually they had plenty of meat. All the men were excellent hunters—some of them real experts. The country abounding in game, they kept the forts well supplied with venison and bear-meat.

Hunting, however, at this time was extremely hazardous, the woods being alive with Indians; but the hunters always kept a sharp look-out. So well trained and accustomed to forest life were they, that they could pass through the woods as noiselessly as the Indians.

When considered at all admissible to venture outside the fort to labor, the men went in company, taking their trusty rifles with them. While some performed the work, clearing the ground, making rails, building fence, or plowing, as the case might be, others stood alternating as sentinels to watch for the approach of their savage foe. They worked one day on the land of one man, and the next on that of another, and so on till they got round.

The women of those days were "helps" meet for

their husbands, willing to endure any privation, and assist them in the performance of any labor. Some of them could handle the rifle with great skill, and bring down the game in the absence of their husbands, especially when, as was often the case, the deer made their appearance near the cabin. They would have shot an Indian, if need be, without a moment's hesitation. At the commencement of the war of 1812-1813, a fort was built at the cabin of George Smith, about two miles from where the city of Richmond now stands. All the families of the neighborhood moved into this fort. At one period, when the alarm caused by Indian depredations had measurably subsided, the men ventured out to work without their rifles. One day they were all at work about a mile from the fort. In the afternoon the dogs from the fort commenced a fierce barking in the thick woods on the path leading to the spot where the men were at work. The women concluded there were Indians in ambush there, waylaying the path for the purpose of massacring their husbands on their return from work in the evening. They held a council and determined to go out and reconnoiter, and if Indians were there attack them and drive them away. They selected one of their number to act as captain, and another one to stay with the children and open the gate of the fort to them in case they were driven back by the Indians. They formed in the fort, each woman taking her husband's gun, shot-pouch, and hunting-knife, then marched out in single file. On reaching the woods a short distance from the fort they deployed to the right of the path and entered the spice-bushes, which grew so thickly a beast could scarcely get through them. They proceeded cautiously, the captain a little in advance of the skirmish line. Advancing slowly, they reached the place where the dogs were, and discovered that they were barking at some Indian ponies. Reconnoitering till satisfied that there were no Indians there, they ventured out into the path, marched back to the fort, and hung up their guns.

Many incidents might be recorded showing the bravery of the women who assisted their husbands in clearing away the forest in Indiana and in contending with the red men of the woods. Here is another one: There had been quite an alarm at the fort for several days, caused by signs of Indians observed by the hunters while out in search of game. The alarm caused the men in the fort to increase their vigilance. For several days and nights they kept sentinels constantly posted, expecting an attack. While some stood as sentinels the others slept with their guns in their arms, ready for action at a moment's warning. A few nights had passed and no assault was made. Their fears began measurably to subside. One night the men placed on guard, being overcome from loss of sleep, lay down at their port-holes, and were soon utterly unconscious. Every one in the fort, save Mrs.

Smith, who was watching with a sick child, was sound asleep. A little after midnight some dogs that had been left outside the fort commenced a furious barking at the far side of a small meadow, in the edge of the woods, full twenty-five rods distant from the fort. Mrs. Smith went to the sentinels and found them asleep. She made some effort to awake them, but they were not easily aroused. She concluded to go out and reconnoiter and see if she could ascertain what the dogs were barking at. The night was quite dark, there being no moon and but little starlight. She opened one of the gates of the fort and passed out. Moving stealthily along under the shadow of a fence till she reached the woods, then slowly and cautiously approaching the place where the dogs were, she discovered that they were baying some animal which fled at her approach. She returned to the fort, passed in, refastened the gate, and watched with her sick child till morning, when she related her exploit, telling the men if she had been an Indian she could have massacred them all while they slept.

In the first settlement of the country, from the dimness of the paths which led from one settlement to another, and the density of the forests, the people frequently lost their way and became bewildered. It was not uncommon to hear at night the cry of some one lost in the woods. Most of the settlers kept a trumpet. When the distant cry of some one so lost in the forest was heard at a cabin, the trumpet was blown as a signal to the bewildered that they were heard, and for them to direct their course thither. In the stillness of the night one hallooing in the woods would be heard at a great distance. Sometimes persons were lost for a day and night, and now and then some were lost and *never* found.

Miss Patsy Odell started one afternoon on horseback to go from one settlement to another some nine miles distant. Night coming on before she reached her destination, she lost the path upon which she was traveling. The night was dark, and the undergrowth in the woods was so closely matted that it was difficult for her to make any headway. After striving for some time to regain the path, finding herself completely bewildered she gave it up as a hopeless case; she hallooed at the top of her voice for a long time, but she was too far from any human habitation to be heard. At last she was brought to realize that she was lost in the wild woods, and would have to spend the night alone. Wolves were howling around her in every direction. Her greatest care now was to find, if possible, some place where she might be secure from them. After wandering about in the darkness for a time she came upon a high log; she succeeded in getting from her horse to the top of it, where she sat, holding him by the reins till morning. When morning came she could determine nothing as to her whereabouts or what course to steer to find a settlement. She sat upon the log ruminating on her forlorn condition till the sun had mounted high in the heavens. At length she concluded to try her horse, and see if he would take her out of the wilderness. Accordingly she remounted and gave him the rein. He wandered about for some time, appearing to be in a maze. At last he struck upon a course, and after traveling some miles brought her out safely at her father's cabin.

Some persons when lost in the woods soon become so frightened as not to be able for a time to recognize their most intimate friends. Those who have never suffered the experience can scarcely form an idea of the terrible feeling, the dreadful fright that comes upon a person when lost in the wilderness. In some instances the lost one has become partially wild in a short space of time. In 1810 a lady on the frontier, in what is now Wayne county, had her cabin on the outside of the settlement, near the land belonging to the Indians. She had been to a neighbor's cabin on an errand and started for home a little before sundown. Night closed in, however, before she was in sight of her home, and the darkness became so dense that she could not follow the path. In a short time she became so confused that she knew not which way to go. This caused her great alarm. She commenced calling for help, her terror increasing every moment. Her husband, who had grown uneasy at her stay, started out on the path with a torch to meet her. Hearing her calling at some distance from the path, he answered her, but she was so much alarmed that she did not recognize his voice, and made off in an opposite direction, thinking the voice she heard was that of an Indian. Her husband pursued her as rapidly as possible, still calling. He could hear her running through the bushes, which enabled him to follow her. The flight and pursuit having been thus continued for some distance, her husband overtook her, when she gave up, supposing she was captured by an Indian. So frightened was she that she was trembling from head to foot, and did not recognize her husband till he took hold of her. Her alarm at finding herself lost deprived her of self-possession.

CHAPTER X.

CHRISTOPHER RODDY.

We do not present the subject of this sketch as a pious man, nor because of his great worthiness, but to show the sternness of character possessed by some of the men who first settled Indiana. Christopher Roddy was a very wicked man, but having been a Revolutionary soldier was honored and treated with respect by the people. He sometimes drank spirituous liquor to excess, and he had indulged in profanity and other wicked practices till he was hardened in sin. He had fought through the whole seven years of the Revolutionary war. During his long service in that war he had contracted his habits of profanity and intemperance. He was so wicked the pious had but little hope of his ever becoming religious, of his salvation. The most of them gave him up as a hopeless case.

The writer will never forget the impression made upon his mind in his boyhood when, while some pious acquaintances were conversing with Mr. Roddy and endeavoring to persuade him to cease sinning and to seek God in the pardon of his sins, he exclaimed: "It is of no use; there is no salvation for me. I believe my damnation sealed as surely as if I was now in hell." This startled the men who were talking with him. They inquired the reason of his so expressing himself. He answered: "Time was when I had a desire to be saved—when I went to the place of worship; I loved to go there—when my heart was melted under the preaching of the Gospel—when I could shed tears at human sorrow and woe—when I felt the drawings of God's spirit and desired to get to heaven; but, for ten long years I have had no desire to be religious; for ten long years I have not visited the place of worship, and have no desire to do so; for ten long years I have had no tender emotion, no tears have dropped from my eyes, however great the sorrow of those around me, nor have I felt the drawings of God's spirit. I do n't *want* to go to heaven. God knows the flames of hell will be a refuge for me if they *will but hide* me from his presence." While the old man uttered these fearful declarations his eyes seemed to flash *fire*, and every muscle in his body *quivered*.

Does not this case show that there is a point in sin beyond which one may go whence there is *no* return? Yes, there *is* danger of judicial abandonment. This man's great wickedness consisted in his profanity and intemperance—in having slighted offered mercy and resisted the strivings of the Holy Spirit, and in "Treasuring up unto himself wrath against the day of wrath, and the revelation of God's righteous judgment."

Mr. Roddy emigrated with his family to the Territory of Indiana, and settled in what is now Wayne county in the year 1810 or 1811. He was considered an honest man, though, as before stated, a very wicked one. He was capable of enduring a great amount of fatigue—was far removed from cowardice—was never known to quail before an enemy or danger—was somewhat eccentric, and always accomplished what he undertook if it was within the range of possibility.

While Roddy was a non-commissioned officer in the army of the Revolution, on one occasion he gave a mortal affront to a second lieutenant who challenged him to fight a duel. By the "code of honor" the challenged party had the right to choose the weapons, the place, and mode of fighting. Roddy accepted the challenge, and chose a heavy cavalry saber for his antagonist and a shoemaker's pegging awl for himself. The place of fighting was to be a large brick oven. The fight was not to commence till both were fairly in the oven. The idea was so novel and ridiculous that his antagonist withdrew the challenge, abandoned the fight, and there the matter ended.

Not long after the county-seat of Wayne county had been removed from Salisbury to Centerville, a colored man by the name of Pitt was convicted for murder and condemned to be hung. After sentence was pronounced Pitt engaged another colored man, by giving him his horse, to take charge of his body after he was executed, he seeing that it was decently interred. This colored man secured possession of Pitt's horse, and then, in advance of the execution, sold his body for ten dollars to two physicians for the purpose of dissection, and left the country. This fact came to the knowledge of Pitt while confined in prison. He sent for Roddy and requested him to take charge of his body after execution, and not to let the physicians have it. Roddy agreed to do so, and pledged himself to Pitt that his wishes should be faithfully and sacredly regarded. When the day of execution arrived Roddy was on hand with a coffin, upon a sled, and the physicians were on hand with a wagon, without a coffin. When Pitt's dead body was cut down from the gallows by the sheriff, Roddy seized hold of it and so did the physicians. A long and hard struggle ensued, but Roddy triumphed. He took the body away from the physicians, put it in the coffin upon his sled, and conveyed it to his home in Salisbury, where he guarded it through the night. The next day he buried it. Fearing the physicians would find out where the interment had taken place, he disinterred the body the next night, removed it from the coffin and carried it on his shoulder some seven miles and buried it in the woods. The next day he cut down all the forest trees he could make fall on the grave, and left it under that mass of timber. He kept his word, and the physicians never obtained possession of the body. Such was Roddy's determined character; such his perseverance in whatever he undertook. Had he embraced religion in his youth and lived a pious life he might have accomplished good, and might have died in peace, but his life was a stormy one, his old age melancholy, and the day of his death dark.

CHAPTER XI.

THREE FRIENDS.

W. C., J. J., and T. C. were pioneers in Indiana, and settled contiguous to each other. Having been born and brought up in the same neighborhood, in one of the old States, they formed an attachment for each other in boyhood, which continued through life. Unfortunately all three grew up to manhood without religious training or restraint. They were taught to be honest and industrious, nothing more; the truths of Christianity were spoken of by their associates in youth only in derision; hence, in riper years, they had respect neither for religion nor religious people. They were men of rugged physical frames, brave and daring, kind and accommodating to their frontier neighbors. Not allowing themselves to be brought under religious restraint, they had no reverence for the Divine Being. The race of these men was short. The youngest of the three, T. C., was called first to struggle, single-handed and alone, with the grim monster. His attack was sudden, the disease malignant and rapid in its progress. He was soon brought down to death's door. When eternity, with all its dread realities, was just before him, he was awakened to a sense of his condition.

He saw hell opening to receive him, his sins rising like mountains to heaven, and calling loudly for Divine vengeance, while the frowns of the Almighty, red with wrath, were poured upon him. He was greatly alarmed. The agony of his mind was such as to cause him to lose all sensibility of his physical sufferings. His whole care was how he might "escape the death that never, never dies."

Though unused to prayer, he called mightily upon God for mercy. One or two pious women pointed him to the Savior, as well as they could, and poured out their souls in earnest supplication to God that he would have mercy upon him and save him from dropping into the bottomless pit.

This dying man now warned his two friends, who were with him to administer to his bodily comfort, that their infidel notions were false, that their course in life would not do, and besought them to lead new lives and prepare for death.

Struggling in deep penitency and earnest prayer for some hours, a great change was wrought. Suddenly he commenced praising the Lord, declaring that he felt his sins forgiven, and was now ready to depart. Though his sufferings had been such as to reduce him to great weakness, when this change took place his strength revived. He arose from his bed, despite the efforts of his friends to prevent him, and walked the room, praising God, declaring what great things he had done for him, exhorting all in the room to prepare for death. When his strength failed, and he could continue no longer, he laid down upon his bed again, and in a few moments his voice was hushed in death.

This made some impression upon the two surviving friends. They were much astonished at the closing hours of their departed companion, but did not change their course in life nor renounce their infidelity.

A short time after the death of T. C., one of the other two, J. J., was suddenly taken ill, and in a few days closed his eyes in death. After he was attacked with disease he was much disturbed in mind. When he saw himself just on the bank of the river that separates time and eternity, he had feelings such as he had not experienced before. His sentiments in regard to man's accountability to his Maker underwent a great change. He renounced his infidelity, and sent word to his friend, W. C., that "Paine's Age of Reason," and other infidel writings, had been his ruin, and besought him to cease reading them. He died, however, without making any profession of religion, leaving to his friends no well-grounded hope of his future bliss.

It was not long after the death of J. J. till the other friend, W. C., was attacked with a lingering disease, which brought him slowly down to the grave. During his long-continued suffering he had much time for reflection. He dwelt much upon the death of his two former friends, the strange change wrought upon one, his rejoicing in a dying hour, and the last solemn message sent him by the other. It was a hard struggle for him to give up his infidel principles; it was hard for him to consent to die—to pass into a world to him unknown, one about which he had thought but little during the whole course of his life. But death was inexorable. Step by step he was brought down to the cold stream. When standing upon the margin, just ready to dip his feet in Jordan's waters, he gave up his cherished principles, and acknowledged man's responsibility to his Maker. He manifested a desire to converse on the subject of religion. On one Sabbath day several persons had called to see him, among them Mr. B., who had been an associate of his for some years. In their conversation the sick and dying man informed his friend of the struggle of mind he had passed through, and that he had renounced his former principles, assuring him that he now believed man was an accountable being, and would have to give an account to God for all his actions in this life. Mr. B. still contended for their old infidel notions. The conversation continued till Mr. C., finding his strength failing, and perceiving he had made little or no impression upon his friend, with deep emotion said: "Well, my friend, when you are brought low down upon a death-bed, you will then know who rules; you will not think *then* as you do *now*." Here the conversation ended.

Mr. W. C. lingered about one year from the time he was taken ill. He made no profession of Christianity before his death. In the prime of life these three friends were taken away, each leaving a young family. Some of their children are yet living, respected. A son of one of them is now in the Congress of the United States.

We have introduced these three men as a warning to parents and young men. They were honest, industrious citizens, but wicked men, and wielded a bad influence upon those with whom they associated. Had they been trained religiously—had good seed been sown in their hearts in early life, and had they shunned infidel authors, the probabilities are they would have lived useful lives, died happy deaths, and found a home in heaven. The happy death of the one is but a manifestation of God's amazing mercy, and not to be taken as an encouragement to procrastinate repentance to a dying hour.

Parents, "train your children in the nurture and admonition of the Lord." Young men, avoid reading infidel books as you would deadly poison.

CHAPTER XII.

GEORGE JULIAN.

THE subject of this sketch was a native of Virginia, born and brought up among the mountains. His education was limited. Having been reared among the mountains, accustomed to much physical exercise, he was, when in his prime, a man of great muscular power. He was early trained to hunting, and became so skilled in taking game that none surpassed him in that department of a mountaineer's life. No man loved adventure more than he. He was always in his element when in the woods with his gun and hunting apparatus. We have heard him say, the happiest days of his life and the best living he ever enjoyed were, when all alone among the mountains of Virginia he was bear-hunting. He would take his knapsack filled with corn-meal, a little salt, his gun, tomahawk, and hunting-knife, go into the mountains and spend two weeks alone. He would kill a fat bear, bring it in to his camp in the evening, take off the skin, spread it upon the ground with the flesh side up, pour some corn-meal upon it, put in some salt, mix the meal with the oil upon the skin without the use of water, then put the dough in the fire and bake it. While his bread was baking he would cut out some of the choice pieces of the bear, salt them well, put them upon sticks, and place them before the fire to roast. When his bread was sufficiently baked he would take it from the fire. Upon this and his roasted bear-meat he made his supper. This, he said, "was the best dish any man ever partook of." He was converted and united with the Methodist Episcopal Church when a youth, and lived and died a faithful member. He emigrated to the Territory of Indiana in 1809, and settled in what is now Wayne county. He was advanced in life when he emigrated. He was of great service to the inhabitants of the fort built in the neighborhood where he settled. Though all the men were good hunters, he was chief among the chiefest. He seldom failed to bring down his game when he fired his faithful rifle.

He was a sweet singer, able in prayer, and a good class-leader. On funeral occasions, Grandfather Julian, as he was familiarly called, frequently officiated—there being no minister residing within many miles. The usual services on such an occasion were singing and prayer at the house before starting to the grave, and as the procession marched to the place of interment, an appropriate hymn was sung, and at the grave another hymn, in which all joined, followed by prayer. On one occasion, at the funeral of a child, Mr. Julian sung a hymn so exceedingly appropriate that some Friend-Quakers who were present thought he composed it by inspiration as he proceeded.

Some years after the close of the war, a circumstance occurred which involved the old man in deep sorrow, and compelled him to give up his little home, where he had fondly hoped to have spent the remnant of his days. A son, an only child by his second wife, grew up a bad boy, indulging in many vicious habits. When this son was about seventeen years of age, three of his associates were spending a Sunday afternoon with him at his father's house, his parents being from home. Young Julian left the three boys standing in the yard and entered the house, closing the door after him. In a few moments one of the boys, whose name was Owens, left the others and started to pass through an open space between the house young Julian had entered, and another which stood near by. As he was entering the open space he saw young Julian with a gun presented—the door being partly open—as if about to shoot. Before he could say "do n't shoot," the gun discharged, and he fell pierced by a ball which entered his side, passing into his bowels. As soon as the gun fired, young Julian pitched it into the loft of the cabin, and ran out, saying: "I thought it was nothing but a wad." Young Owens lived till the next morning, when he expired. Young Julian was arrested and thrown into jail. When court came on he was indicted for murder. The father employed General James Noble, one of the ablest lawyers in the State, to defend his son. The State's attorney was James B. Ray, then in his prime, who was afterward Governor of Indiana. The case was ably conducted on the part of the prosecution and the defense. The plea of "accidental shooting" was put in on the part of the defense, and on that ground the jury acquitted young Julian. The old gentleman had to sell his home to pay the fees of his lawyer and other incidental expenses attending the trial. He then moved to Flat Rock, in Rush county, where he ended his days. He did not long survive this affair, which brought his gray hairs down to the grave with sorrow. He was a good man, respected by all who knew him.

CHAPTER XIII.

METHODIST EXHORTERS.

At an early day in Indiana exhorters were of great service to the Church. They held meetings on the holy Sabbath, and often at night during the week. They were remarkably efficient in conducting prayer meetings and in leading the classes. They frequently held two days' meetings. On these occasions no attempts were made to preach, but instead, exhortations of live, burning pathos were delivered that told with marvelous power upon the hearts of the people. Preachers being scarce, the settlers were glad to have the exhorters come among them and lead their devotions. Their usual manner of conducting a two days' meeting was to have two or three stirring exhortations in quick succession, then to set out a "mourner's bench," invite penitents forward and go into a general prayer meeting. Almost always the shouts of new-born souls were heard before these exercises closed. On Sabbath morning a general class meeting was held. These were "times of refreshing from the presence of the Lord." At these class meetings, and on love-feast occasions, a door-keeper was appointed who admitted none but members of the

Church and those who were truly serious on the subject of their salvation. Persons not Methodists were always conversed with at the door by the door-keeper, and if found penitent, and would promise to conform to the rules of the love-feast or general class meeting, were admitted, provided still further that they had not enjoyed the privilege more than two or three times, or if they had would now promise to unite with the Church. These meetings were select. The pious, when thus separated and shut in from the world, felt at liberty to speak freely of their Christian experience, all being in sympathy one with another. While one was speaking, fervent prayer was ascending from all in the house. Then were hearts melted, then did their hearts glow and burn with sacred fire. Here the strong were made stronger, the weak were strengthened, and often penitents were converted. Of these times and places many could sing:

> "O sacred hour! O hallowed spot!
> Where love divine first found me;
> Wherever falls my distant lot
> My heart shall linger round thee."

The exhorters who assisted in building up the Methodist Church in Indiana were a pious and useful class of men. They filled their places in Immanuel's ranks well, and deserve to be remembered.

There were no Church periodicals in those days in which to publish obituary notices of those who fell with their armor on. Many of them now sleep in forgotten graves, with no stone to mark the spot where their ashes repose, but their record is on high. We will present brief sketches of a few of them:

Hardy Cain was a fine singer, and did much to move and melt the hearts of the people by his songs. His voice was musical. He was also very able in prayer, successful in laboring with penitents, faithful and gifted in exhortation. He was useful as an exhorter, and in that capacity did much good. In this exercise, as soon as he began to grow warm, he commenced rubbing his face with his hands. As his feelings arose he would grasp his ears with both hands and then pour forth his soul in exhortation in such a way as to affect the whole congregation. In class meeting he was in his element. Few men were more successful in leading than he. After exercising his gifts as an exhorter for a number of years he was licensed to preach, and filled the place of a local preacher, and continued otherwise a faithful toiler in his Master's work, till he was called home to receive his reward.

James Honley was a man of fine appearance, and had a voice of trumpet tone. He could be heard at a great distance, and his tones always fell pleasantly on the ear. His exhortations were uniformly solemn, and produced a deep impression upon the heart and mind. The people heard him with delight. He was exemplary in his life, steadfast in piety, respected by the people, and did much good.

Though but an exhorter, he will, doubtless, have stars in the crown of his rejoicing.

Mr. Miller was a man of small stature, of quick motion, and very zealous in all his religious devotions. He had a clear, shrill voice, which sometimes seemed to electrify the people. When he prayed, the heavens were opened and streams of salvation came down upon the congregation. His countenance indicated that he was a man that lived near the foot of the cross—one who held constant communion with the Father, Son, and Holy Spirit. He was pathetic in exhortation, moving his hearers to tears. He has long since crossed the river and entered into rest. His son, Rev. Charles W. Miller, has been an itinerant Methodist preacher for twenty-six years, and is now a member of the North Indiana Conference.

Spencer.—This brother, though a mulatto, is worthy to be named and remembered. He was born a slave, and was compelled to wear the galling chain till some time after he had grown to manhood. He was known by one name only—*Spencer.* His mind, naturally strong, would have shone with brilliancy, had the advantages of education been his. Despite, however, the crushing *slave power*, he could read, and had acquired quite a fund of knowledge. By the blessing of a kind Providence he was liberated from bondage, and at a very early day came to Indiana with some of his friends, who settled in Wayne county. No exhorter, in all the region round about, was more popular than Spencer. He had a talent for the work of a high order. The people were glad at all times to see him make his appearance among them when met for worship. He was often called upon to exhort after the traveling preachers had preached. His voice was most melodious—sweet as the sound of the *dulcimer*. He would sometimes set a whole congregation on fire by singing one of his favorite songs, such as,

> "Hark! listen to the trumpeters!
> They sound for volunteers;
> On Zion's bright and flowery mount
> Behold the officers!"

> "Hark! brethren; do 'nt you hear the sound?
> The martial trumpet now is blowing,"

And

> "Sweet rivers of redeeming love
> Lie just before my eyes."

He seldom failed to move and stir the congregation. Sometimes the tide of feeling rose so high that his voice was drowned in the general rejoicing of the people. Many years since, after a long and painful illness, his sufferings ended, and in holy triumph he bade the world adieu.

John Doddridge.—Mr. Doddridge emigrated to Indiana when it was a Territory. He settled in what was afterward called "Doddridge's neighborhood," six miles south of Centerville, Wayne county. He was not a learned man, but a very successful exhorter, and full of the Holy Ghost. He was always on hand at quarterly and two days' meetings, ready to act his part. He delighted to labor with penitents, and few had greater success in that particular work. Being deeply experienced in the things of God he knew well how to point the heavy-laden to the Lamb for sinners slain.

A large and flourishing class was organized in his neighborhood, and a log meeting-house erected which was known far and near as Doddridge's meeting-house. For several years camp-meetings were held on his land. On these occasions he was always in the front rank of Immanuel's host. His voice, as he shouted to the onset, could be heard high above the noise of the battle. After he had resided in Indiana ten or fifteen years he received intelligence concerning a sister older than himself, but whom he had never seen. She had been captured in Virginia by the Indians when a small girl, before he was born. The Doddridge family had received no tidings of this lost child from the period when she was carried off till now. They supposed she had been dead many years. When Mr. Doddridge received information of her being still alive he went to the Indian nation and saw his sister. She was now old, and had lived so long among the Indians that she would not leave them and return to her relatives.

John Doddridge was a good man, and "fought a good fight, finished his course," and has been crowned with eternal life.

CHAPTER XIV.

MORAL HEROINES.

There were many pious females among the early settlers who were Christian *heroines* in the true and full sense of the word. Having left their native States and accompanied their husbands to the Territory, when it was nought but a howling wilderness, they had proved themselves to be helpmeets for the men who braved the dangers of a frontier life. Not only were they resolute to endure the hardships and privations to which they were exposed in the wilderness, from ferocious beasts and cruel, savage men, but were equally bold in the Christian warfare. They were ever found by the side of their husbands on every moral battle-field, fighting for the Lord. Many of them could sing with a voice that, in its heavenly sweetness, never failed to charm the ear and melt the heart. While their "hands held the distaff," or while they plied the shuttle or the needle, their voices were tuned to sweetest melody.

They were neither ashamed nor afraid to pray in the public congregation. Though they felt the cross, they boldly took it up and bore it aloft in the sight of all the people. When they drew near to God in prayer, and by faith took hold of the horns of the altar, heaven opened, light shined, salvation came down, and the gates of hell were made to tremble. Women who cultivate their talents are peculiarly gifted in prayer; this seems to be their special calling. We have heard some women pray with an eloquence and power surpassing any thing that ever fell from the lips of man.

These moral heroines usually accompanied their husbands to two days' and quarterly meetings. Some of them thought it no hardship, after having performed their daily toil, to walk four miles along an Indian-trace to a week-night prayer meeting. They delighted in the privileges of the class-room. When mourners were at the "mourner's bench" these faithful women were among them pointing them to the Savior of sinners. In love-feasts they acted well their part. One after another they would arise, and stand with streaming eyes and glowing countenances while they spoke of their penitential sorrow; of the joyful hour when first they felt a Savior's pardoning love; of the deliverances God had wrought out for them; of how religion had sustained them when called to leave, in a distant land, the graves of loved ones, and make their homes in the wilderness, and then of their prospects of joining the blood-washed throng in the land of light and bliss, where there shall be no more sighing. These holy mothers so deeply impressed themselves upon their sons and daughters that their memory will "be ever fresh and green."

The authorities of Indiana have published the "Roll of Honor," giving the names of those brave men who went forth under the stars and stripes to fight for their country in the late cruel, bloody rebellion. These moral heroines are equally worthy of having their names recorded in the history of the Church in our State. They were the mothers and grandmothers of many of the brave boys who so nobly stood for the right against treason in the hour of their country's peril.

But these mothers have nearly all passed away. Only a few linger on these mundane shores. A few years more and the last one of them will be safely housed in their "home beyond the tide." The old class-papers upon which their names were inscribed are lost, and we have no record of them left; nevertheless, their names are written in the Lamb's book of life, and the roll will be called when Adam's long line shall be assembled at the judgment-seat of Christ.

CHAPTER XV.

PROGRESS OF METHODISM IN THE STATE.

In the year 1819 the work in Indiana was so arranged as to place the circuits in two Annual Conferences, namely, the Ohio and Missouri, and to form three districts, namely, the Lebanon and Miami, in the Ohio Conference, and the Illinois in the Missouri Conference. There were three new circuits formed, which appear upon the Minutes this year for the first time, namely, Madison, Indian Creek, and Harrison.

The circuits were placed in districts as follows: Whitewater in Lebanon district, with Moses Crume presiding elder; Lawrenceburg and Madison, in Miami district, with John Sale presiding elder; and Silver Creek, Indian Creek, Blue River, Harrison, Vincennes, Patoka, and Pigeon, in Illincis district, with Jesse Hale presiding elder.

Allen Wiley and Zachariah Connell were sent to Whitewater circuit, Benjamin Lawrence to Lawrenceburg, John T. Kent to Madison, David Sharp to Silver Creek, William Mavity to Indian Creek, John Pownal to Blue River, William Medford to Harrison, John Cord to Vincennes, John Wallace and Daniel M'Henry to Patoka and Pigeon. This was a year of considerable prosperity. The whole number of members in Indiana was three thousand four hundred and seventy, giving an increase, for the year, of four hundred and twenty-six.

In 1820 the districts and circuits were again changed, and supplied as follows: Miami district, Ohio Conference, Walter Griffith presiding elder; Whitewater circuit, Arthur W. Elliott, Samuel Brown; Lawrenceburg, Benjamin Lawrence, Henry S. Fernandes; Madison, Henry Baker, William H. Raper; Indiana district, Missouri Conference, Samuel Hamilton presiding elder; Silver Creek circuit, Calvin Ruter, Job Baker; Indian Creek, John Shrader, John Everheart; Blue River, John Stewart, Joseph Pownal; Patoka, John Wallace; Vincennes, Daniel M'Henry. Pigeon and Harrison do not appear on the Minutes this year.

This year Calvin Ruter commenced his labors in Indiana. He had been admitted into the Ohio Conference two years before, and was now transferred to the Missouri Conference. The whole number of members returned this year was four thousand three hundred and ninety-nine, giving an increase of nine hundred and twenty-nine. In 1821 Charlestown, Bloomington, Ohio, Mount Sterling, and Corydon, appear upon the Minutes as heads of circuits. The presiding elders continued upon the districts as they were the past year. This year James Jones was sent to Whitewater, John P. Durbin and James Collard to Lawrenceburg, Allen Wiley and William

P. Quin to Madison, Calvin Ruter and William Cravens to Charlestown, John Scripps and Samuel Glaize to Blue River, Daniel Chamberlin to Bloomington, Job M. Baker to Vincennes, Elias Stone to Patoka, John Wallace to Ohio, George V. Hester to Mount Sterling, and John Shrader to Corydon. The aggregate membership for this year was seven thousand, three hundred and fourteen. Methodism was now advancing rapidly in the State.

In 1822 Allen Wiley and James T. Wells were sent to Whitewater, Henry Baker to Lawrenceburg, James Jones and James Murry to Madison, with Alexander Cummins for presiding elder. James Armstrong was sent to Charlestown, George K. Hester to Flat Rock, John Wallace and Joseph Kinkade to Blue River, John Cord to Bloomington, David Chamberlin to Honey Creek, John Stewart to Vincennes, James L. Thompson to Patoka, Ebenezer Webster to Mount Sterling, John M. Baker to Corydon, and William Cravens to Indianapolis, with Samuel Hamilton for presiding elder. Indianapolis now appears upon the Minutes as the head of a circuit for the first time.

At the present writing, 1866, there are five Methodist preachers and one missionary stationed in Indianapolis, and the charges in the city belong to four Annual Conferences. The borders of Methodism had rapidly enlarged. The men into whose hands the work had been committed were fully devoted to their calling.

In 1823 the number of circuits had increased to fifteen. Two new ones had been formed, Connersville and Eel River. Cummins and Hamilton were continued as presiding elders. The appointments of the preachers were as follows: Whitewater, Russel Bigelow and George Gatch; Lawrenceburg, W. H. Raper; Madison, J. Stewart and Nehemiah B. Griffith; Connersville, James Murry and James C. Taylor; Charlestown, James Armstrong; Flat Rock, Dennis Willey; Blue River, William M'Reynolds and George K. Hester; Bloomington, John Cord; Honey Creek, Hackalia Vredenburgh; Vincennes, John Ingersoll and Job M. Baker; Patoka, Ebenezer T. Webster; Mount Sterling, Stephen R. Beggs; Corydon, James L. Thompson; Indianapolis, James Scott; Eel River, William Cravens. The whole membership this year was seven thousand, seven hundred and thirty-three, giving an increase of four hundred and nineteen.

In 1824 John Strange was sent to the Miami district as presiding elder, John Everhart and Levi White to Whitewater circuit, W. H. Raper and John Jaynes to Lawrenceburg, John F. Wright and Thomas Hewson to Madison, Aaron Wood to Connersville.

William Beauchamp was sent to the Indiana district, Missouri Conference, as presiding elder. Samuel Hamilton and Calvin Ruter to Charlestown, Thomas Rice to Flat Rock, William Cravens and Dennis Willey to Blue River, James

PROGRESS OF METHODISM.

Armstrong to Bloomington, Samuel Hull to Honey Creek, Edward Smith to Vincennes, William Medford to Patoka, George K. Hester to Mount Sterling, James L. Thompson to Corydon, Jesse Hale and George Horn to Indianapolis, and John Cord to Eel River. The whole number of Church members returned by the preachers this year was eight thousand, two hundred and ninety-two—an increase of five hundred and fifty-nine.

In 1825 the Illinois Conference, having been organized, embraced the whole of the State of Indiana. Five new circuits had been formed, and appear upon the Minutes for the first time, namely, Rushville, Salem, Paoli, Boonville, and Mount Vernon. The work in Indiana was placed in three districts: Madison, Indiana, and Illinois. Mount Vernon was the only circuit in Indiana placed in the Illinois district.

John Strange was presiding elder of Madison district, James Armstrong of Indiana, and Samuel H. Thompson of Illinois. The preachers appointed to the circuits this year were as follows: Madison, Allen Wiley and Aaron Wood; Lawrenceburg, James Jones and Thomas S. Hitt; Whitewater, Peter Stephens and N. B. Griffith; Connersville, James Havens; Indianapolis, John Miller; Flat Rock, Thomas Hewson and James Garner; Eel River, John Fish; Charlestown, James L. Thompson and Jacob Varner; Corydon, G. K. Hester and Dennis Willey; Salem, Samuel Low and Richard

Hargrave; Paoli, Edward Smith; Boonville, Orseneth Fisher; Patoka, William H. Smith and George Randle; Vincennes, Edwin Ray; Honey Creek, Samuel Hull; Bloomington, David Anderson and John Cord; Mount Vernon, William Moore.

James Havens, John Miller, Richard Hargrave, William H. Smith, and Edwin Ray appear in connection with the work in Indiana this year for the first time. James Havens and Edwin Ray have finished their work, and are gone to their rest; the others survive. The whole number of members. this year was 8,900, an increase of 610.

In 1826 considerable change was made in the arrangement of the work. There were four districts, and two stations were made, namely, Madison and Salem. These were the first stations formed in the State.

It was a great mistake for the perpetuity of the itinerant system to make stations. It would have been better for the Church in America if we had adhered to the circuit system, like our fathers in England. Stations lose their sympathy with circuits, and circuits with stations. The station system tends to do away with the office of presiding elder. Stations make it necessary to place many fields of labor in one district in order to give the presiding elder a sufficient support without being burdensome to the people. This causes his services to each field of labor to amount to but little, and the quarterly meetings to fail of creating that interest they formerly did. To place a minister in charge of but one congregation, and retain him with *that* for three years, and keep him in the same city for *half a lifetime*, is itinerancy but in *name*. Some sister Churches have as much without the name. If we have no stations, nothing but circuits, as in England, the number of fields of labor in each district should be so reduced as to enable the presiding elder to give a Saturday and Sunday to each quarterly meeting, and at his quarterly visits he could spend three or four days among the people, if need be, and have as many members to draw his support from as under our present arrangement.

This year the preachers were appointed to the work as follows: Madison district, John Strange, presiding elder; Madison station, Samuel Basset; Madison circuit, George K. Hester; Lawrenceburg, James L. Thompson; Whitewater, James Havens; Connersville, Nehemiah B. Griffith; Rushville, Stephen R. Beggs; Flat Rock, James Jones, Thomas S. Hitt; Indianapolis, Thomas Henson.

Charlestown district, James Armstrong, presiding elder; Charlestown circuit, Allen Wiley, George Randle; Corydon, Samuel Low, George Lock; Paoli, John Miller; Bloomfield, Eli P. Farmer; Eel River, Daniel Anderson; Crawfordsville, H. Vredenburg; Bloomington, Edwin Ray; Salem station, William Shanks; Salem circuit, John Cord.

Wabash district, Charles Holliday, presiding elder; Honey Creek, Richard Hargrave; Vincennes,

Aaron Wood; Patoka, James Garner, Joseph Tarkington; Boonville, William H. Smith.

Illinois district, Samuel H. Thompson, presiding elder; Mount Vernon, Orseneth Fisher. It will be perceived that the work was extending northward in the State. Crawfordsville was the most northern circuit, and Mount Vernon was in the extreme southern portion. The total number of members this year was 9,872.

In 1827 the districts and circuits in Indiana were manned as follows: Madison district, John Strange, presiding elder; Madison station, Calvin W. Ruter; Madison circuit, James Scott, Daniel Newton; Lawrenceburg, James L. Thompson, George Randle; Whitewater, James Havens, John T. Johnson; Connersville, Robert Burnes; Rushville, N. B. Griffith; Flat Rock, Abner H. Cheever; Indianapolis, Edwin Ray.

Charlestown district, James Armstrong, presiding elder; Charlestown circuit, Allen Wiley, James Garner; Corydon, George Lock, Samuel Low; Paoli, William H. Smith, Smith L. Robinson; Eel River, Daniel Anderson, Stith M. Otwell; Crawfordsville, Henry Buell; Bloomington, Aaron Wood; Salem, William Shanks, John Hogan; Washington, William Moore.

Wabash district, Charles Holliday, presiding elder; Vincennes, S. R. Beggs; Patoka, Asa D. West; Boonville, Thomas Davis; Mount Vernon, Thomas Files.

PROGRESS OF METHODISM. 115

The total membership this year was 10,740, an increase of 868.

In 1828 the districts remained about as they had been the year previous. Some slight changes had been made in the arrangement of circuits and stations. Lawrenceburg was a station this year, being the third one organized in Indiana. The appointments of the preachers were as follows: Madison district, John Strange, presiding elder; Madison station, Edwin Ray; Madison circuit, James Garner, A. H. Chever; Lawrenceburg station, J. L. Thompson; Lawrenceburg circuit, Allen Wiley, D. Newton; Whitewater, T. S. Hitt, James Scott; Wayne, S. R. Beggs, William Evans; Connersville, Robert Burnes; Rushville, James Havens; Columbus, C. B. Jones; Indianapolis, N. B. Griffith; Vernon, Henry Buell.

Charleston district, James Armstrong, presiding elder; Charleston circuit, George Lock, Enoch G. Wood; Corydon, J. W. M'Reynolds, S. Low; Paoli, William Moore, James M'Kean; Eel River, W. H. Smith, Benjamin Stephens; Crawfordsville, E. P. Farmer; Bloomington, D. Anderson, S. M. Otwell; Salem, William Shanks, John Hardy; Washington, Thomas Davis.

Wabash district, Charles Holliday, presiding elder; Vincennes, John Miller, Ashley Risley; Patoka, Charles Slocum; Boonville, William Mavity; Mount Vernon, Thomas Files. The total number of members returned at the close of this year amounted to

12,090, showing the highly-gratifying increase of 1,350.

We have now given a brief sketch of the progress of Methodism in Indiana for the second decade. In twenty years from the time Methodism was introduced into the State, the number of members had increased to 12,090. In the first twenty years, by the working of the itinerant system, 127 traveling Methodist preachers were connected with the work and took part in spreading Scriptural holiness over these lands. They laid the foundation of the Church deep and broad. We are indebted, under God, to the men who cultivated this field for the first twenty years for the present prosperous state of the Church in every part of Indiana.

A few of these men are still in the active work. Most of them have joined their fellow-laborers where there is rest from toil.

CHAPTER XVI.

POLITICS.

In the early settlement of Indiana, what is now called party politics was a thing unknown among the people. The people had but few political principles, and these were simple and easily understood. When a man aspired to office, the great questions with the people were, "Is he capable? is he honest?" They considered the ballot-box the palladium of their liberties—its purity—something to be guarded most sacredly. If any man had attempted to corrupt the ballot-box by stuffing, or by incorrectly counting, or by procuring illegal votes, or by attempting to buy votes in any way, he would have so completely blasted his reputation, that there would have been "none so mean to do him honor." He could not have found admittance into respectable society. It would have placed a mark upon him that would have made him an outcast. A good reputation was worth something to a man in those days.

Caucuses and conventions to nominate candidates for office were unknown. Every man who so desired declared himself a candidate for office. Sometimes there were ten or twelve candidates before the people for the same office. Every voter selected his candidate and cast his ballot for whom he pleased.

The people did not call themselves after political parties, as Democrats, Whigs, Republicans, etc., but after their respective candidates, as Hoover men, Lomax men, Beard men, Hill men, Pennington men, Test men, Holman men, etc. In the great presidential campaign, when John Quincy Adams, Andrew Jackson, Henry Clay, Thomas H. Crawford, and John C. Calhoun were candidates, the people in Indiana called themselves Adams, Jackson, Clay, Crawford, or Calhoun men, according to their preferences among the candidates. The friends of Andrew Jackson were especially proud to call themselves Jackson men.

On election days, when the people came to the polls to vote, they did not inquire where they could obtain Democratic, Whig, or Republican tickets, but men were passing through the crowd of voters shouting ever and anon: "Here's Jackson tickets!" "Here's Adams tickets!" "Here's Clay tickets!" etc.

Stump-speaking was not practiced in Indiana for several years after she became a State, but was finally introduced and soon became general. At present, stump-orators are numerous. The stump is a great resort for *demagogues*. The people are often misled by its fulminations. Party politics were unknown in the State till after John Quincy Adams was elected President by Congress over

General Jackson. From that period party politics began, and have continued, sometimes running to great excess. The friends of Jackson organized themselves under the title of *Democrats*, and those of Adams under that of *Whigs*. The Democrats carried the State in every State and Presidential election, till the Whigs took it from them under the leadership of General Harrison. After his death, the Democrats took the State from the Whigs, and kept it till the Republicans carried it under the leadership of the immortal Lincoln in 1860. After party politics was introduced into Indiana, trickery was soon resorted to in conducting our election campaigns, even down to the little county offices. These campaigns were not always conducted exactly upon the principles of honesty, but upon the plan most likely to succeed, without regard to whether it was right or not.

In 1840 the Whigs adopted the *raccoon* as their *insignia*, and the Democrats the *rooster* as theirs. The Whigs were led to take the "*coon*" in consequence of the taunts thrown at General Harrison, their candidate for the Presidency. He was called by the Democrats "the log-cabin candidate," "an old hunter," etc. The Democrats were led to adopt the "*rooster*" in the following way: The contest between the two parties in Hancock county was close, and the Whigs seemed to be gaining. Joseph Chapman, a leading Democrat in that county, wrote to one of his political friends in another part of the

State informing him how the parties stood, and asking advice as to what he should do in order to carry the county for the party. His friend wrote back to him to appear in good spirits—to represent the party as gaining, saying to him in the letter: "Crow! Chapman, Crow!" Somehow, the Whigs obtained knowledge of the contents of that letter. Their stump-orators rang the changes on "Crow! Chapman, Crow!" In every Whig gathering you would hear the shout, "Crow! Chapman, Crow!" The Democrats determined to make capital out of these taunts, and adopted the "*rooster*" as their insignia.

In 1842 Joseph Chapman and Thomas Walpole, a Whig lawyer who then resided in Greenfield, were opposing candidates for the State Senate. Walpole had been in the Senate, and Chapman in the House of Representatives. The Senatorial district was composed of the counties of Hancock and Madison. The canvass became warm. The candidates stumped the district together. Walpole was neat in his apparel, and wore ruffled shirts. Chapman was peculiarly slovenly in his appearance. In those days the Democrats charged the Whigs with being the "Ruffled-Shirt Gentry." By this they made many votes among the yeomanry of the country. Upon this charge Chapman rung the changes well against Walpole, as they met upon the stump from time to time, often pointing to the ruffles in his bosom as evidence of the truth of the charge.

They had spent some two weeks in Madison county, speaking every day except Sunday. All this time Chapman had not changed his linen, and it had become so much soiled that even *he* could not endure it any longer. He told Walpole one evening that he would be under the necessity of going home, in order to get a clean shirt, and could not be with him the next day. Walpole objected, and proposed to lend him one. Chapman said, "That will *not do*. Your shirts have *ruffles* on them, and you know I am *fighting* the 'Ruffled-Shirt Gentry.'" Walpole said to Chapman, "You can button your double-breasted vest over your bosom, and hide the ruffles." He consented, and the next morning put on one of Walpole's shirts. That day it was Chapman's turn to speak first. In his speech he reiterated the old charge of "Ruffled-Shirt Gentry," and pointed to the ruffles protruding from Walpole's bosom. When he closed his speech, Walpole arose and with great indignation referred to the abuse he had received from Chapman during the canvass for wearing ruffled shirts. Said he, "Fellow-citizens, I *do* wear ruffled shirts; you see them *now* in my bosom. I am an *honest* man. I do not *try* to conceal them. I *abhor* a hypocrite. What character is so much to be *despised* as that of a hypocrite? This dishonest, hypocritical opponent of mine has been abusing me from day to day for wearing ruffled shirts, and I have borne it patiently, refusing to expose his hypocrisy. I will expose him now, and prove to you that he wears ruffled shirts as well as I." At that moment he caught hold of Chapman's vest, as he sat near him, and tore it open, when out popped a bosomful of ruffles. At this, the audience raised a tremendous shout. Chapman was so much surprised and confused that he did not dare to get up and confess that he had on Walpole's shirt. This trick gained several votes for Walpole.

On the Saturday before the election, which was to come off on Monday, they were speaking in a certain neighborhood in Hancock county, where some vote Walpole had given in the Senate, the Winter before, was very unpopular. Chapman labored to make all the capital he could for himself out of the vote. In order to avoid the force of the arguments Chapman made against him, Walpole positively denied having given such a vote. Chapman pledged himself to the people, that if they would meet him in Greenfield on Monday, the day of the election, he would, by the journal of the Senate, prove that Walpole *did* give that vote; if he did not he would decline the canvass and not ask them to vote for him. The next day he rode to Indianapolis and procured a copy of the Senate journal; on Monday morning he came into Greenfield and put up at Gooding's Hotel; he went into the room he usually occupied, laid the journal upon the table, and walked out on the street. Walpole, seeing him pass out, went into the room, and taking up the journal, found the page where the *hated vote* was recorded, tore it out, put it in his pocket, laid down the journal and went out. When the citizens had generally gathered in town, Chapman returned to the hotel, got the journal, went out, mounted a block and commenced making his speech. Referring to the dispute between himself and Walpole, he renewed his pledge, telling the people he would prove that Walpole had given the vote and was then *mean* enough to deny it. Turning over the pages of the journal he could not find it, not remembering upon which one it was recorded. He became so much confused that he did not discover that the journal had been mutilated. He at last gave up the search under much embarrassment. Walpole then mounted the block, denounced Chapman as a *liar* and a *slanderer*, and demanded that he should decline being a candidate, and called upon the people to vote for *him*.

The result was Walpole was elected. They were both shrewd, talented men, well matched. In the cases related, Walpole obtained the advantage of Chapman.

Political parties tend to corruption. Whenever the people allow themselves to be compelled to vote for a candidate because he has been nominated by a party, their liberties are greatly endangered. No man should vote for a candidate simply because he belongs to the party. Honesty, purity of character in a candidate, is of greater value to the people than the mere profession of a certain set of political principles. Whenever the moral men of the country let the party-political wireworkers know that party politics alone can not command their votes, then those who control and manage political nominating conventions will give them moral men to vote for.

CHAPTER XVII.

MRS. SARAH SMITH.

WE present the following sketch of Mrs. Smith, written by Rev. G. C. Smith, of the South-Eastern Indiana Conference, and published in the Western Christian Advocate in 1854, it being better than any thing we can write:

Sarah Smith was born October, 1776, in the State of Virginia, and died January 10, 1854, in the seventy-eighth year of her age. For more than fifty-two years she was a faithful, consistent, and devoted member of the Methodist Episcopal Church, and lived in the conscious enjoyment of the comforts of Divine grace.

How agreeable soever it might be to surviving friends, and how desirable soever for the instruction and encouragement of others, that the pious and useful life and high Christian character of this now sainted "mother in Israel" should be spread out in detail before the public eye, the writer may decline the office of furnishing such *desideratum*. She was his mother; but for the praise of God's glorious grace he can not forbear to offer the following brief outline, deeming this as slight a tribute as a grateful son may well consent to pay to the memory of such a mother. "A woman that feareth the Lord, she shall be praised." "Her children shall rise up and call her blessed."

When a small child she was left an orphan with an elder sister, by the death of both her parents. She was then taken by a kind uncle, who brought her up as one of his own family. When a little over twenty years of age, she was united in marriage to George Smith. The marriage was solemnized on New-Year's day, 1797, in Union district, South Carolina, where they both then resided. With him she had lived, at the time of her death, more than fifty-seven years in uninterrupted harmony and conjugal felicity. She was indeed a helpmate. Never did woman more nobly and fully sustain that office. Through all the vicissitudes of life—in the gloomy paths of adversity, and in the sunny walks of prosperity—she was ever the same sympathizing, affectionate, and devoted companion. With grace and ease she could enter into the cares and recreations, the joys and sorrows of her husband. In her domestic relations she made it her study to smooth the asperities and enrich the felicities of life.

Some five years after her marriage she became religious, and joined the Methodist Episcopal Church. She was one of the happy thousands who were brought to experience salvation in that wonderful revival of religion, which occurred about the close of the last and the beginning of the present century, and which extended all over the Southern and then

Western States. During that remarkable period of religious excitement, camp meetings were introduced—those public means of grace by which, in modern times, so often hundreds, if not thousands, as on the day of Pentecost, have been "turned from darkness to light, and from the power of Satan unto God," and "added to the Church in one day."

The first of these meetings held in that part of the country was in 1802. The spot selected was a pleasant grove in the valley of Inoree River. Here, in the midst of the most picturesque scenery, the hundreds who came pouring in from every direction, some from the distance of fifty miles, pitched their tents in irregular clusters. Soon were gathered together a vast multitude; people of all grades and conditions, high and low, rich and poor, black and white, Methodists and Presbyterians. Here, far from the noise and bustle of the crowded city, surrounded by a landscape clothed in nature's richest drapery, midway between those lofty hills which rose along on either side of the river, and overlooked the valley; and while, as introductory, the songsters of the grove were chanting their mellow notes, the congregation of religious worshipers commenced their devotions. Fervent prayer was offered up. The Word of God was delivered at three different stands at the same time, in living thoughts and burning words, "in demonstration of the spirit and of power;" and soon the groans of the sin-sick arose, and mingling with the shouts of the redeemed, went booming up the valley, and echoed from hill to hill. The voice of joy and praise broke forth from the tabernacles of the righteous, and the noise was heard afar off, while the placid waters of the gentle river glided by in silence, as if listening at the sound. Had Balaam stood on some one of those hill-tops which skirted that valley, looked down upon those tents as they stood spread out through the grove, and heard the joyous sounds of salvation as they rose from the encampment, and rolled along the banks of the quiet Inoree, surely he would have exclaimed, as when, on the hights of Pisgah and Peor, he stood beside the son of Zippor, and saw the camp of ancient Israel spread over the plains of Moab, "How goodly are thy tents, O Jacob; and thy tabernacles, O Israel! As the valleys are they spread forth: as gardens by the river side! The Lord their God is among them, and the shout of a king is among them."

At this camp meeting hundreds were smitten by the power of Gospel truth, and fell to the ground under the preaching of the Word; hundreds, too, receiving the spirit of adoption, were then and there happily converted to God.

At this meeting the husband of the subject of this sketch was powerfully convicted, and was converted on his way as he went home. She, with him, soon after, joined the Methodist Episcopal Church. Some time after this, while her husband was at family prayer, she experienced converting power; 'twas bright as noon; she was unspeakably happy. Then she realized what Wesley sung:

> "My God is reconciled,
> His pard'ning voice I hear;
> He owns me for his child,
> I can no longer fear."

These lines she ever afterward held in the highest estimation, and often repeated them with all the deep emotion and holy confidence with which their author was inspired when first he sung them. From that happy hour she never doubted her acceptance with God. Through all her Christian warfare, which lasted over fifty-two years, she "fought a good fight, and kept the faith." Though she passed through scenes of trial and conflict, she never wavered in her attachments and fidelity to the Church and the cause of religion. Her trust in God was strong and steady. It is confidently believed that she never spent a day in all her long life, after her conversion, without some bright manifestation of Divine grace. She seemed always to be conversant with death, and in sight of heaven, to stand day by day on Pisgah's top. She was exceedingly fond of singing such words as, "O Jesus, my Savior, I know thou art mine." "Sweet rivers of redeeming love lie just before mine eyes."

The resurrection of the body was a subject which she contemplated with the most triumphant emotion. Often has she seemed to exult in such unearthly ecstasy in anticipation of that glorious consummation of Christian triumph, as utterly to confound the unbelievers. When, singing one of her favorite hymns, she came to the words, "Arrayed in glorious grace shall these vile bodies shine," her soul would sometimes take wing, and, rising from the world, would soar for awhile amid the scenes of the upper sanctuary.

In prayer she was truly gifted. In this she possessed uncommon power. Though she was not an educated woman, her prayers were remarkably fluent and often eloquent. She was wonderfully successful at the altar among penitents. If their convictions appeared not sufficiently pungent, she would lead their minds in a train of such full and earnest confession and loathing of sin and wickedness as to make them shrink and cry for mercy; then pouring forth her intercessions in their behalf, she would raise them on the arms of faith, and standing at the very throne would present them for mercy with such assurance in the appeal, "Jesus, Master, now fulfill thy sacred word, as thou hast said, Blessed are they that mourn, for they shall be comforted," as rarely failed of success.

Many happy souls will rejoice in eternity that they ever met this saint of God at the altar of prayer. Often at the social prayer meeting, when all seemed cold and lifeless, she has been called on to lead in prayer, when soon the Holy Ghost has been shed upon the people, and the shout of victory has gone up from God's altar. Her prayers at the family altar will never be forgotten by her children. Many, many a time have they wept under her impressive prayers, while parents and children kneeled together at the domestic altar.

For many years before her death she enjoyed the blessing of perfect love. She loved the Lord and she loved the Church. She would sing with peculiar zest as expressive of the feelings of her heart:

"I love thee, my Savior; I love thee, my Lord;
I love thy dear people, thy ways, and thy Word."

A true and warm friend to itinerant ministers, her house was, for fifty years, their home. She was always glad to see a minister of the Lord Jesus enter her habitation, and felt unfeigned pleasure in ministering to his comfort. Many a weary itinerant has found a cordial welcome at her threshold. Never was she frustrated or confused in her domestic arrangements by the unexpected appearance at her door of these men of God, but she always continued to render them easy and comfortable, as if their visit had been in pursuance of a special invitation. Indeed, it was with her substantially as with the Shunamite, who, in the days of Elisha, had a chamber on the wall furnished with a bed, and table, and stool, and a candlestick, for the prophet of the Lord as he passed that way, that he might turn in and rest. Among those who enjoyed her Christian hospitality may be mentioned a Crume, a Finley, (Robert,) a Strange, a Cummins, a Bigelow, a Griffith, a Wiley, etc. These are some of the sacred and honored dead, but many yet live in whose hearts her memory is embalmed by the recollection of the itinerant's home.

In the Spring of 1809 she, with her husband and five children, emigrated from South Carolina to Indiana, in the then far West. They settled in Wayne county. Their residence was on the very borders of civilization, being just one mile from the Indian lands. Hundreds of wild savages were roaming through the neighboring forests. These were frequent guests, generally very troublesome—often terrible to lonely families on the frontiers. When hungry they would call and demand something to eat, and the family that neglected to supply their demands was almost sure to incur their displeasure, sometimes their revenge.

During the British and Indian war of 1812-1813, the white inhabitants for some miles around united together and constructed a fort at her residence for their common protection against the violence of their savage neighbors. The fort consisted of a small piece of ground inclosed by a thick line of palisades in the form of a square. These palisades were made of the trunks of trees, split into slabs three or four inches in thickness, and twelve or fourteen feet in length, set upright, with one end in a ditch cut three feet deep, thus furnishing a wall some ten feet high. Within this inclosure a suitable number of houses were built for the accommodation of the resident families. Into this fort the neighbors repaired in time of alarm and danger. Though the tribes in that part of the country were not professedly engaged in the war which was being waged against the country, yet considerable mischief was done in the neighborhood of the fort, such as stealing, and even murder.

Religious services were kept up in the fort. Occasionally they had circuit preaching. Once in a while the itinerant minister would find his way to this fort. Sometimes he bore upon his shoulder a musket to defend his life against the savages. Sometimes he carried in his hands a hatchet to mark his way, that he might subsequently retrace his steps.

The subject of this sketch was remarkable in her attentions to the sick. These she did not suffer herself to neglect. Around the couch of the afflicted she would linger with the most unremitting care, glad to do a kindness, ever ready to minister to their comfort and spiritual instruction. Being herself feeble in her constitution, and much afflicted during her life, she knew well how to sympathize with the sick. She saw six of her children laid in the grave, four of them in infancy. She murmured not. She believed that her Savior took her infants, and she saw the adult ones enter Jordan in the triumph of faith. The four children left behind her cherish in their hearts a sacred reverence for her pious life.

About twelve years before her death she made a

request of her youngest son, in relation to her funeral. She asked him to see to having sung at her burial the hymn commencing,

"And must this body die?"

and to have her funeral sermon preached from the words, "Be ye also ready; for in such an hour as ye think not, the Son of man cometh." These circumstances considered alone may seem to possess no interest, but when viewed in connection with her life and death, they present coincidences which are somewhat remarkable. Her life was distinguished for that constant readiness which befits one whose departure from the world was to be sudden and unexpected. She died at the residence of her son of whom she made the request, just six weeks from the time she arrived at his house, and her remains are interred at Orleans, Orange county, Indiana. She died without a moment's warning, in the presence of several of her friends. She left without a sigh, not even a long breath. Thus sweetly and swiftly she passed from earth to the paradise of God.

CHAPTER XVIII.

GEORGE SMITH.

OF the subject of this sketch, the following has been furnished us by a friend:

George Smith was born January 21, 1777; he died July 11, 1857. The place of his nativity was Union district, South Carolina. His ancestors were of the purest Anglo-Saxon blood. Their distinctive religious faith was that of the "Society of Friends," commonly called "Quakers." Some of the more remote ones were among the earliest members of that religious society. According to the best genealogical and biographical data available, they emigrated from England to America in company with the famous William Penn, and originally settled in Pennsylvania. After some years, that branch from which George descended removed to South Carolina. His father and mother were both zealous and prominent Quakers, the latter of whom was a reputable preacher in that denomination. In the time of the American Revolution, his parents, in common with many of their countrymen, suffered much from the predatory incursions of the numerous Tories who infested that part of the country. More than once their residence was assailed and plundered by those political banditti of the most valuable portable articles. On one of these occasions, in the absence of his father, his mother's life was providentially preserved from the violence of these military robbers. Having entered the domicile and commenced their depredations, one of them, an officer, seized a favorite household article which she held in her hand, and after a short, ineffectual struggle to wrest it from the grasp of the brave woman, he aimed a furious blow at her head with his sword, which struck the upper ceiling and glanced aside from its object.

Both his parents died, the one a few years after the other, while he was only fourteen years of age. Left thus so early an orphan to struggle through life, without the protection and guidance of parental hands, he found in his own native energy and firmness of purpose the elements of power sufficient, under the Divine blessing, to sustain him and to conduct him triumphantly through that most critical juncture, his minority. In the true spirit of domestic heroism he went to work, took the younger members of the family under his care, and made all necessary provision for their temporal comfort during the time of their needed guardianship.

Having arrived at a suitable age, he was married to Sarah Kennedy, with whom he lived in the happiest union for fifty-seven years and ten days. She went before him to the spirit-land about three years and a half. Her death was the great bereavement and affliction of his long life; but the grace of God sustained him. After he grew to maturity he apostatized from the religion of his fathers, or, rather, declined personally to embrace its peculiarities; yet he never ceased to adhere, with the greatest tenacity, to the great moral principles of the Gospel, as held and taught by them. Consequently, he never ranged among the profane and wicked of that day.

In 1802 he was converted to God, and became a member of the Methodist Episcopal Church. At the first camp meeting held in that country, and the first which he ever attended, he was deeply convinced of sin. He mourned as a penitent, and sought the Lord with prayers, strong crying, and tears. During the services the power of God was displayed in a wonderful manner, particularly on the holy Sabbath. On that day the people—hundreds of them—lay prostrate on the ground, like men slain in battle, insomuch that the scene appeared awfully grand.

Under a sense of the wrath of God abiding on him, his feelings became so intensely excited that he could not consent to remain all the day upon the ground, but in the evening left for home. On his way thither he turned aside to pray, and while alone, agonizing in prayer, the Savior spoke his sins forgiven and his soul rejoiced in the conscious enjoyment of acceptance with God. He never afterward doubted his conversion. On his return home the same evening he erected the family altar, whose fires he never suffered to become extinct for a day, nor even to decline, till, after the lapse of more than fifty years, he became so aged and helpless that he was unable to stand upon his knees to pray. A short time after his conversion he had the joyful pleasure of witnessing the clear and happy conversion of his companion while he was leading the devotions of family prayer.

In the Spring of 1809 he took his family, which consisted at that time of his wife and five children, and emigrated to the then far West. He stopped his team and unpacked his goods in an almost unbroken wilderness, at a point a little north and about two miles west of where the ctiy of Richmond now stands, in Wayne county, Indiana. That was then on the very outskirts of civilization, all the lands west of him being claimed and occupied exclusively by the red men of the forest. Here he pitched his tent and commenced opening out a farm, little he and the few neighbors around him thinking of the vast and rapid tide of population and enterprise which was to sweep over the western wilds within fifty years from that day. But he lived to see, in less time than that, the wilderness give way and the flourishing capital of Indiana standing seventy miles west of the spot where his frontier tabernacle stood, with her twenty-five thousand inhabitants, her grand State-house, her noble asylums, and her spacious and beautiful churches. He lived to see the boundary of civilization, which lay within a mile of his habitation, rolled westward till it reached the shores of the Pacific. In the place of his border settlement he resided for many years.

After some brief arrangements for the temporal accommodation of his family, his next great care was to seek for the enjoyment of Christian privileges. During the first Summer after his arrival in that wilderness land, the pioneer Methodist preachers found their way thither, and preached a few miles from his log-cabin. At the first news of their approach he started and met them at the place, introduced himself, gave the names of himself and wife as members of the Methodist Episcopal Church, and invited them to his humble dwelling. They came, and it was not long till his own cabin was made a preaching-place; a class was formed and he appointed leader. Many years from that date his house was constantly and emphatically the itinerant Methodist preacher's home. There many a weary minister rested, and rallied his recuperative energies for further toils in his Master's vineyard.

Few men were living at the time of his death, who were citizens of Indiana when he came to this country. It was then known as the Indiana Territory. Few, indeed, were the settlements made within the limits of what is now Wayne county, the most populous part of the State. All, or nearly so, of his early neighbors had died and gone before him. In the social etiquette of a new country all are recognized as neighbors, who live within ten or fifteen miles of each other. In that country and in those days Methodists walked, after the toils of the day, from one to five miles to prayer meeting at night. In simplicity, sincerity, and earnest Christian zeal—not fanaticism, as some have called it—they met, and sung, and prayed, and shouted for an hour or two, in some humble, but honored private habitation. The services having been concluded, while the fire of unsophisticated, soul devotion yet glowed in their hearts, and while their eyes were yet moist with the waters of pure, spiritual joy, they gave each other a frank, hearty, and friendly greeting, ardent enough to singe the mossy faces of the fossilized Christians of the latter days.

Soon there might be seen numerous brilliant torches blazing and gleaming in sundry directions through the dense forest, as these worshipers wended their way to their respective log-cabin homes. Those shining torches were fit and significant emblems of that inner light and fire of spiritual devotion which they carried in their hearts. Often it happened that sin-sick souls were healed along the way, whose new song of praise and shouts of joy made the dark caverns of the wilderness vocal, and sometimes sent the wild beasts in affright and haste from their nightly slumbers.

The men of that day were confessedly inferior to our cotemporaries in the fine arts of Church polity. They were less skilled in the polemics which relate to family-sittings, choir-singing, theological schools, etc.; but in the discussion and maintenance of the truth, or the greater and more vital subjects of experimental religion, justification by faith, the witness of the Spirit, humble obedience to Christ, according to the simple, old-fashioned theology of Wesley and Fletcher, "there were giants in those days." One could chase a thousand, and two could put ten thousand to flight of the pulpit-performers, tame sermonizers, Sunday lecturers, Gospel-diluters, and dulcifiers of other days.

The subject of this sketch commenced early in his Christian life the systematic study of the Holy Scriptures, accompanied by prayer and meditation. This faithful reading of the Word of God gave him a more thorough knowledge of the things revealed than men ordinarily possess. The Bible was distinctly *his* book to the last. He had read the Old and New Testaments regularly through many times in succession. This course of reading he continued till a few months before his decease, when his sight had so far failed him that he had to give up this enjoyment. This privation he keenly felt. He often, however, called on his friends around him to read for him. He had read much in the theological works of his day. Wesley, Fletcher, Clarke, and Benson were his favorite authors. He had read Dr. Clarke's voluminous Commentary—every word in it—that was written in the English language. In Methodist theology he was critical—ready to detect any variations, no matter how slight, from the standards of the Church. He was particularly tender and affectionate toward young ministers, and yet he managed, without seeming captious, often to suggest to them improvements in their sermons. He passed through all the shades and grades of frontier life. The privations, hardships, and sufferings incident to a new country became familiar to him. These he encountered and withstood in the prime and vigor of his life. When old age and infirmity came upon him, his own country had passed into a high state of cultivation, and, to some extent, had developed her rich resources. Owing to infirmity, a few of his last years were spent without the enjoyment of the public means of grace. He was unable to attend the sanctuary.

After the death of his companion, with whom he had walked to the house of God for fifty-seven years, he was, much of the time, lonely. His great desire was to depart and be with the Lord; yet he would often repeat and apply to himself the language of Job, "All the days of my appointed time will I wait, until my change come." His heart was in heaven; his mind was staid on God. During the last two or three months of his life he kept his eyes closed much of the time; and, when asked for the reason, he invariably answered, "There is nothing in this world upon which I desire to look. When my eyes are closed, I am looking by faith to heaven, where Jesus is, and where my departed friends are."

A few days before his departure, while alone in his room, and about the hour of midnight, his soul was greatly blessed. While rejoicing, his son, with whom he resided, awoke from sleep, and hearing the voice of joy went into his father's bed-chamber and found him unspeakably happy. For some hours he continued in a strain of praise to God. He said he had never, in all his life before, been so happy.

For more than three years he lived with his youngest son, Rev. W. C. Smith. During that time he buried the companion of his youth. And so attached was he, afterward, to the spot where she was laid, and the very soil which covered her remains, that he often said, "*There* is the place where I wish to be buried."

He trained up his children in the nurture and admonition of the Lord. They all became religious, and joined the Methodist Episcopal Church. Four only of his children survived him. These are on the way to Zion. Two of them are ministers of the Lord Jesus. He was a citizen of Indiana more than forty-eight years. George Smith was proverbial for honesty, integrity, firmness, and piety. During a membership in the Methodist Episcopal Church of fifty-five years, he rendered efficient service in various relations. Throughout nearly the entire length of the active portion of his life, he was a class-leader, or a steward, or both.

At the house of his youngest son, in the city of Indianapolis, a few minutes before six o'clock, in the afternoon of July 11, 1857, in the eighty-first year of his age, he sweetly fell asleep in Jesus, and was gathered, like a ripe shock of corn, into the garner of heaven. According to his request, his mortal remains were interred by the side of those of his companion. There they rest together in hope of the resurrection.

CHAPTER XIX.

REV. MOSES CRUME.

The subject of this sketch was one of the first itinerant Methodist preachers who labored in Indiana. Rev. Mr. Williams had preceded him the year before. Rev. Hector Sanford accompanied him when he came to the Territory in 1809.

It is unfortunate for the Church that so little is known of the talents and worth of these holy men of God, who came as pioneer ministers into the wilds of Indiana. Their appointments from year to year are found in the Minutes of Conference, but that does not give the extent of the fields of labor they cultivated, the hardships they endured, nor the battles they fought, nor the victories they won, under the Great Captain of their salvation.

Rev. Moses Crume was, perhaps, born in the State of Virginia; at least he was born, the second time, in that State. He was awakened and led to the foot of the cross, through the instrumentality of *father Hathaway*, who traveled Berkley circuit, in 1785. He emigrated to Kentucky, where he was licensed to preach at a quarterly meeting held at Ferguson's Chapel, April 12, 1793. In 1808 he was admitted on trial into the old Western Conference, which held its session that year at Liberty Hill, Tennessee, and was appointed to Whitewater circuit, Indiana, with H. Sanford for a colleague. This circuit, at that time, embraced all the settlements in the Territory, from the Ohio River extending north. The most northern appointment was Meek's Meeting-House, on Clear creek, in what is now Wayne county.

In 1811 he was returned to Whitewater circuit, without a colleague. This year he extended the circuit still further north, and established an appointment at the cabin of George Smith.

In 1814 Mr. Crume was appointed to Lawrenceburg circuit. This was the third year he had labored among this people, Lawrenceburg circuit having been stricken off from the Whitewater circuit.

In 1817 he was appointed presiding elder of Miami district, which he traveled two years. Lawrenceburg and Whitewater circuits were embraced in this district. The other years of his itinerant life were spent in the State of Ohio.

Mr. Crume was a man of noble bearing; his countenance was grave; his appearance in the latter part of his life truly patriarchal. His hair he wore long, after the old style, parting it upon the top of his head, and combing it back behind his ears. His appearance in the pulpit was commanding; his voice was mellow and deep-toned. He could hardly have been called an orator, but he was logical. He did not move and stir the feelings of an audience, but seldom failed to make an impression for good. He never indulged in fancy, but presented the truths of the Gospel in a plain, simple form, such as convinced the mind of the hearer. He was an expounder of God's Word. His manner of presenting the truth was such as to impress the minds of those who heard him, that *he* felt and believed what he taught the people.

No one ever doubted his piety. His life was such as to impress all who enjoyed the benefit of his acquaintance and association, that he was truly a man of God. This eminent minister of the Lord Jesus is associated with the writer's earliest recollections, and his appearance is photographed upon his memory. Many have blessed God that he ever lived, and in the day of eternity will claim him as their spiritual father.

After a long and useful life, in 1839 he died in great peace at his residence, in the neighborhood of Oxford, Butler county, Ohio.

CHAPTER XX.

REV. JOHN STRANGE.

John Strange was among the early preachers in Indiana. Various sketches of him have been written, but all have failed to present him fully to the reader. Indeed, few pens are competent to such a task. Those who have written of him have each contributed to the perpetuation of his memory. They have spoken of his excellencies, and yet the half has never been told. To know and fully appreciate the worth and talents of this distinguished minister of the Lord Jesus, the people had to see him, form his acquaintance, and hear him preach. The writer does not suppose that his pen can do justice to his exalted character, nor surpass those who have written before him; but he would pay this humble tribute to the memory of one he claims as his spiritual father.

Mr. Strange was admitted on trial in the old Western Conference in the year 1811. At that time the Western Conference embraced the States of Mississippi, Tennessee, Kentucky, Missouri, Ohio, Indiana, and Illinois. The preachers of this Conference were liable to be sent, from year to year, to any part of its bounds. To enter the itinerancy in a Conference of such dimensions, at such a time, required more devotion to the cause of the Redeemer, more of a self-sacrificing spirit, and more courage than men ordinarily possess.

Mr. Strange was a Virginian by birth, and in boyhood emigrated to Ohio with his father. He was not favored in early life with a good education, but he possessed an active, vigorous mind, and a high order of native talent. He could have prepared himself in youth, and at manhood entered upon any one of the lucrative professions, particularly that of the law, and arisen to distinction and affluence; but in early life he had sought and found the Savior, and united with the Methodist Episcopal Church—consecrating himself, time, and talents to the Lord. Hearing his Master's voice saying, "Go ye into the wilderness in search of the lost sheep of the house of Israel," he heeded that voice, and "chose rather to suffer affliction with the people of God than to enjoy the pleasures" of wealth and fame. He bade farewell to worldly prospects, ease, the pleasures of home, and, casting himself wholly upon the Lord, for time and eternity, he entered the itinerant ranks. Having once shoved off from the shore, he never looked back to the day of his death. For twenty-two years he was a houseless, homeless wanderer, preaching Jesus and the resurrection wherever he went. He loved to sing:

"No foot of land do I possess,
No cottage in the wilderness;
A poor wayfaring man.

> I lodge awhile in tents below,
> And gladly wander to and fro,
> Till I my Canaan gain."

Mr. Strange's first appointment was to Will's Creek circuit, in the State of Ohio. His second appointment was to Cincinnati, with the distinguished William Burke for his colleague. In the Fall of 1812 he was sent to Whitewater circuit, Indiana. This circuit was large, embracing all the country from a short distance above Lawrenceburg, north to the headwaters of Whitewater, and west as far as there were any white settlements.

At this time the war with Great Britain and her Indian allies was in full blast. It was exceedingly hazardous for a solitary man to travel through the country; nevertheless, Mr. Strange failed to fill few, if any, appointments. Not believing it was his duty to yield up his life to the cruel savages that infested the country, lurking in every forest and glen, without an effort to defend himself, he procured a trusty rifle, which he carried with him wherever he went, always keeping a sharp look-out for Indians as he passed through the dense woods.

His most northern appointment was at a fort built on Clear creek, two miles north-west of where the city of Richmond is now situated. At this fort he made his appearance every four weeks, with his rifle upon his shoulder. Here, on each visit, he usually spent two or three days ministering to the inhabitants. These visits afforded great consolation and encouragement to those who were thus shut up in the wilderness.

In the Fall of 1813 Mr. Strange was appointed to Oxford circuit, in Ohio. In 1814 he was sent to Lawrenceburg circuit, in Indiana. In the Fall of 1815 he was returned to Ohio, being appointed to White Oak circuit, which he traveled two years. In the Fall of 1817 he was sent to Mad River circuit. To this circuit he was returned the next year. In 1819 he was sent to Union circuit, where he remained two years. In the Fall of 1821 he was appointed presiding elder of Lebanon district, in Ohio. The next year he was sent to Milford circuit. In 1823 he was appointed presiding elder of Miami district. This brought him back into Indiana—Lawrenceburg, Whitewater, Madison, and Connersville circuits being in his district.

The next year Illinois Conference was formed, and all the work in Indiana was placed in that Conference. Madison district was formed, and Mr. Strange was appointed to it. He continued to travel this district for the next four years, when he was appointed presiding elder of Charlestown district. He remained upon this district three years, when the Indianapolis district was formed, and he was appointed to it. At the close of his first year as presiding elder of that district, he was compelled to take a superannuated relation. His slender frame could no longer endure the hardships and privations he had been undergoing. The toils and labors he had been performing on large circuits and districts for twenty-two years, in a new country, were too severe for him. This was his *last* field of labor. It was a hard struggle for him to consent to give up the active work, for his soul still burned with holy zeal for the salvation of precious souls, but he yielded with the best grace he could.

It is said that a gentleman who greatly admired Mr. Strange deeded him a quarter section of wild land, as a token of his high regard. Mr. Strange kept the land a short time. Feeling that the land encumbered his mind, and abridged some enjoyments he greatly prized, he went back to his friend and gave up the deed, requesting to be relieved of his burden, stating, that since he had received that present, he had not been permitted to sing his favorite song,

"No foot of land do I possess," etc.,

and could not forego that enjoyment. This may be thought an error in Mr. Strange. If it was, it was one of the head—not of the heart. He had given himself unreservedly—time and talents—all his ransomed powers, to God and the Church, and was afraid to allow himself to become encumbered, in the smallest degree, with worldly goods, lest he should be hindered in the work committed to his hands. His faith was strong that God would provide for himself and family, and supply his wants through life. In this he was not mistaken—he had not believed in vain. So deep was the hold he had upon the affections of the people, that after he superannuated, his friends purchased a house and lot, on the south side of Market, between Meridian and Pennsylvania streets, Indianapolis, and presented it to him. They took great pleasure in supplying his necessities, and administering to his comfort, till he entered into that land where the inhabitants hunger no more, and where the Lamb leads them to fountains of living water.

Mr. Strange was about six feet in hight, of slender frame, hair jet black and very straight, eyes black, clear, and piercing. His form was erect, standing or walking. All his movements were peculiarly graceful—particularly in the pulpit. His social qualities were of the highest order, yet he never failed to maintain his ministerial dignity, without affectation, or the appearance of stiffness. His voice was clear and distinct, sweet and melodious—over it he had perfect command. He could raise it to the highest, or bring it down to the lowest key, without the slighest jar or discord. He was one of the finest singers that ever "tuned a voice to sweetest song." He was very fond of music when in the family circle; and in the public congregation he often lifted the people from their seats, by the power of his song. He could render the hymn commencing,

"Hear the royal proclamation,"

with more effect, perhaps, than any man who ever tried it.

In the pulpit, he was peerless in voice and gesture. No one ever imitated him—for none could. He was a natural orator of the highest class. It was no studied art with him—it was Heaven's rich gift. His power over an audience, at times, seemed to be almost supernatural, causing their feelings to rise and swell, at the command of his voice, or the waving of his hand, as the ocean would surge under the call of Æolus. Often the people were so carried away by his eloquence that, rising from their seats, they would press toward the place where he stood telling the story of the cross—portraying the dying agonies of the Savior—themselves seemingly lost to every subject but the one presented by the speaker.

He was sometimes eccentric in the pulpit, but *his* eccentricities were always graceful. From any other man than John Strange, some of his remarks would, perhaps, have been inadmissible. He possessed what Rev. Mr. Taylor, in his *Model Preacher*, calls "surprise power," in a very high degree. This he used to great effect. By his sudden exclamations, he would thrill a whole congregation as by a shock of electricity. Sometimes, when speaking of God's love to man in the redemption of the world, the joys of Christ's great salvation, the glory of heaven, his soul would be filled with such heavenly rapture, that he would exclaim in his peculiar voice, "Alleluia! Alleluia! Alleluia!" when the people would catch the spirit, and from every part of the congregation shouts of praise would ascend to heaven.

Sometimes, when portraying the torments of those shut up in the prison-house of hell, and describing the wicked as in crowds they urged their way down to blackness and darkness, the sinners in the congregation would scream out, crying for mercy. Seizing upon the occasion, Mr. Strange would exclaim, in his inimitable way, "A center shot, my Lord; load and fire again!" The backwoods hunters knew well how to apply such expressions.

On one occasion, when he was preaching on Sunday at a camp meeting, the tide of feeling rising higher and higher, he took one of his wonderful flights of eloquence, which lifted the congregation, and a general shout arose. Hearing the great shout which rolled up from within the inclosure of tents, a crowd of persons who had been wandering about on the outside of the encampment, came rushing in through an opening to the row of tents, and down the center aisle toward the stand. Seeing the coming throng, Mr. Strange stopped short, raised himself to his full hight, and, standing upon his tiptoes, threw his right hand forward, pointing with his index finger directly toward the crowd, and then exclaimed, in a voice which seemed to startle the people from their seats, "Here they come now! My Lord, shoot them as they come!" At once, scores of loud "amens" rolled up from the congregation. Instantly, as if stricken by lightning, the whole crowd of sinners who were pressing down the center aisle, dropped upon seats, and on the ground. From that moment he held the congregation at his will, till the close of the sermon.

His powers of description were of the finest order. He could so describe a scene, that you would seem to behold, in undimmed light, that which he was portraying. When he was preaching the funeral sermon of Rev. Edwin Ray, in Indianapolis, toward the close of the discourse, while describing the second coming of Christ, his bringing with him "them that sleep in Jesus," descending "in the clouds of heaven," he stood erect for a moment, then, looking upward, cried out, "Where is Edwin Ray?" Still looking upward, he said, "I see him; I see him!" and then, with both hands raised as if welcoming him, he exclaimed, in a voice that seemed to go up to the clouds, "Hail, Edwin! Hail, Edwin! Hail, Edwin!" The effect upon the congregation will never be forgotten by those who heard that sermon and felt the power.

After a lingering illness of pulmonary affection, in holy triumph, in the city of Indianapolis, on the second day of December, 1833, he bade the world adieu, and went up to join the blood-washed throng around the throne of God. When the word, "Rev. John Strange is dead," spread abroad, there was mourning throughout the Church in Indiana. Blessed man! Peace to thy memory!

CHAPTER XXI.

REV. HUGH CULL.

HUGH CULL was among the first, if not *the* first, Methodist local preachers in Indiana. He was one of the pioneers, and took an active part in planting Methodism in the eastern portion of the State. He was a man of so many excellencies, of so great worth, that he is "worthy to be had in everlasting remembrance." As a tribute of respect to his memory this sketch is given.

Hugh Cull was born of Roman Catholic parents, in Havre-de-Grace, Md., October, 1759. When he was four years of age, his father removed to what is called the Red-Stone country, Pennsylvania. Here he continued to reside till he was twenty years of age. In 1777, with his father, he emigrated to Kentucky. They located their habitation where the city of Lexington is now situated. In 1785 he went to Henry county, Kentucky, where he was afterward united in marriage to Miss Rachel Meek, a devotedly pious member of the Methodist Episcopal Church. She was in the sixteenth year of her age.

Though not addicted to many of the vices common to young men in a new country, his training had not been such as to lead him to piety, or incline him to any of the Protestant Churches, particularly the Methodist Episcopal Church. In a short time after his marriage, he was, through the instrumentality of his faithfully pious young wife, led to the foot of the cross, where he found the Savior, and then united with the Methodist Episcopal Church. So thorough was his conversion, so deep his piety, so earnest his zeal, so ardent his attachment to the Church, and such were his talents, that in a short time he was licensed to preach.

From the time he united with the Church his house became a home for the weary itinerant, and continued to be as long as he had a house, which was a period of more than seventy years. Rev. Jacob Young, in his *Autobiography*, speaks of Mr. Cull's house as a "most hospitable home for Methodist preachers."

In 1804 he came to Indiana to explore the country. In 1805 he brought his family out, which consisted of his "beloved Rachel," and Patience, a niece of his wife, whom they had adopted as a daughter. He pitched his tent on the land he had entered, in what is now Wayne county. All around him was one wild wilderness. In a short time his humble cabin was erected, into which he placed his family and erected the family altar, which was never taken down.

Though a man of feeble physical frame, and apparently slender constitution, he opened a farm in the dense forest and supported his family comfortably. There being no other minister of the Gospel residing in that part of the Territory, and the traveling preachers not having yet found their way into that region, it devolved upon Mr. Cull to plant the Gospel-standard. He at once set about the work. He invited the few families that were in reach of him to come to his cabin, stating he would preach to them. He also visited distant settlements on Sabbath days, and established preaching-places. As soon as the itinerant preachers came in reach, he went after them and invited them to his abode. They came and organized a class at his house, and made it a regular preaching-place, which it continued to be for twenty years.

Mr. Cull was a man of medium size, with black hair—till whitened by age—which he always combed back upon his head, heavy eyebrows—neat in his appearance. He had a pleasant voice, mellow in its tones; he had a very fair English education; he possessed the confidence of his fellow-citizens in a high degree. He was a member of the Convention which met in Corydon, then the seat of government for the Territory, and which formed the first Constitution of the State. He was an influential member of that Convention, and took an active part in its deliberations. The people had great respect and reverence for him. He was called Father Cull by the citizens generally, as far back as the writer's memory goes. He was a man of tender heart, strong affections, kind spirit, full of sympathy, of deep unostentatious piety. He had the full confidence of all who knew him. He was mighty in prayer, a man of strong faith, always enjoying a sacred nearness to God when at the throne of the heavenly mercy.

He was a good preacher, zealous and pathetic. The people always heard him gladly. He was a man of tears when preaching, and often the whole congregation would be melted, under his sermons and exhortations. He delighted much in hearing the Gospel preached; on it he fed and feasted. When his soul was filled with joy Divine, he loved to say glory! It seemed to afford him peculiar pleasure. "Glory, glory, glory!" was a common expression of his, when in an ecstasy of joy. He was a warm and true friend of the itinerant preachers, delighting in their society, bidding them welcome to his home; ever ready to assist them to the best of his ability. At an early day he traveled a part of a year, as a "supply," when his circuit extended from Lawrenceburg, on the Ohio River, as far north as Greenville, in the State of Ohio. The country was new, the streams were unbridged, the roads almost impassable; consequently, the traveling was laborious and hazardous. He was always ready to take the circuit for a round or two, when it was necessary to supply the place of a sick preacher, or one who was called away from his work for a short time.

Father Cull resided on the farm where he first settled when he came to Indiana, fifty-seven years ago. He died on the thirty-first day of August, 1862, aged one hundred and four years and ten months. He retained his physical and mental vigor, in a very remarkable degree, to near the close of his long and useful life. About three months before his departure his physical strength began to decline. Gradually he descended to the grave. The taper of life burned lower and lower, till it went out. As his end drew near, the prospect of joining his former friends and companions, and the wife of his youth, who had passed on before, filled his soul with heavenly rapture. The last words that escaped his lips on this side the river, and they came forth in a whisper, were, "Glory, glory, glory!" Thus lived and died Rev. Hugh Cull.

CHAPTER XXII.

REV. JOHN GIBSON.

John Gibson was the second Methodist local preacher who settled in what is now Wayne county, Indiana. He came to the Territory at an early day. Where or when he was born is not known to the writer; nor what were the circumstances surrounding him in early life; nor when nor where he was converted and united with the Church; nor when he was licensed to preach. The presumption is, that he was, in early life, very much after the Benjamin-Abbott style. His education was limited, but sufficient for his station in life and the people to whom he ministered in their wilderness-homes. He was rather uncomely in his appearance, low of stature, very round shouldered, of great muscular power, for a man of his size. He was of sanguine temperament—kind spirited—a true friend—firm in his principles, and fearlessly advocated what he believed to be right, and opposed what he believed to be wrong. He was a *terror* to evil-doers. In his sermons he feared not to charge Satan's strongest holds. The vices of the day met in him a steady and powerful opposer.

He was a man of true piety and of great zeal in

his Master's work—of great faith—a good preacher, always acceptable to the Church, but dreaded by the servants of Satan—very successful in laboring with penitents, and a powerful exhorter. He had some peculiarities. He sometimes used expressions in prayer which would have sounded strangely, coming from the mouth of any other man than John Gibson. On one occasion, at a camp meeting, while a prayer meeting was being conducted in the altar, many persons were seeking salvation, and many souls were being converted, the preacher's stand was crowded with the proud and haughty, who stood looking on. Among them, and at the front of the stand, stood a young woman, very gayly attired, who was making sport in a very derisive manner of the exercises. Mr. Gibson was on his knees in the altar, with his face toward the stand, earnestly engaged in laboring with the penitents. Looking up he saw the young woman laughing and making sport. He suddenly exclaimed, in great earnestness, "My God! knock that young woman down!" repeating it three times; when, as if pierced by a rifle-ball, the young woman fell into the altar. Mr. Gibson turned to a lady who was kneeling near him, and, tapping her on the shoulder, said, "Sister, that is what *I* call taking them between the lug and the horn." This young woman, after a long and hard struggle, was powerfully converted.

Mr. Gibson labored as a local preacher for several

years, and was instrumental in the salvation of many souls. He and his associates in the "kingdom and patience of Jesus" have all gone home to their Father's house above, where, reunited, they join in the song of the redeemed, "Unto him that loved us and washed us from our sins in his own blood, and hath made us kings and priests unto God; to him be glory forever and ever." He died in holy triumph, in Wayne county, Indiana, in the year 1818.

CHAPTER XXIII.

INTRODUCTION OF METHODISM INTO RICHMOND.

RICHMOND, in Wayne county, was originally settled by Friends, commonly called "Quakers." John Smith and Jeremiah Cox, the proprietors of the town, were influential members of that denomination. Some years before Richmond was founded, Whitewater Friends' Meeting-House was built a short distance above the site of the town as first laid out. The town improved rapidly. The inhabitants were principally Friends. From their peculiar religious tenets they did not give encouragement to any other denomination. They were a quiet, moral people, very exact in the observance of all religious duties as held and taught by their own Society. They, at that time, associated but little with persons of other Churches. They seldom, if ever, allowed their houses of worship to be occupied by ministers of other denominations. These they were pleased to call "Lo-heres and Lo-theres," and considered it their duty to warn their people not to run after them. It was several years after the town began to improve before any other religious denomination made an effort to establish themselves in the place. The Methodists were the first. In

1822 Rev. Russel Bigelow was preacher in charge of Whitewater circuit. He determined to make an effort to plant Methodism in Richmond. It was difficult to obtain a house to preach in. The inhabitants who were not *Friends* were by no means friendly to the Methodists. None would open their houses. After a time permission was obtained to preach in a small school-house. In this Mr. Bigelow preached the first sermon delivered by a Methodist preacher in Richmond. He soon organized a small class, consisting of the following persons: George Smith, Sarah Smith, Mercy B. Smith, Rachel S. Smith, Stephen Thomas, Margaret Thomas, and the widow Pierson. George Smith was appointed leader of the little band. It was not long till the school-house was taken from them. Preaching and class meetings were then moved to a small room occupied by the widow Pierson as a dwelling. In a short time after this Mrs. Pierson moved from the town, when the class was discontinued, the other members living in the country and not being able to procure another house to worship in. The town was now given up by the Methodists for a time. In the Fall of 1825 Rev. James Havens was sent to the circuit. During the year he determined to make another effort to establish Methodism in Richmond. A small house in the lower end of the town, remote from any other residence, which was occupied by Isaac Jackson, was obtained, preaching was established and a class organized. From that period Methodism has maintained a place in Richmond.

For several years the Church met with the most decided opposition. The struggle for an existence was a hard one. Satan and the enemies of the Church strove hard to drive her from the place. The faithful few who were there united in Church fellowship, were firm in their religious principles, praying always, "lifting up holy hands, without wrath and doubting," that God would strengthen them, give them the victory, and add to their number such as should be saved. The ministers sent to them from year to year labored diligently, shunning not to declare the whole counsel of God. Gradually, the Church gathered strength, and her membership increased in numbers.

The first Methodist two days' meeting held in Richmond, commenced on the first Saturday in June, 1828. At that time there were but few members in the place, but they were devotedly pious, and were closely united in Christian bonds, though surrounded by the most intense opposition. Rev. Stephen R. Beggs, who was in charge of the circuit, had made the appointment. There had been considerable prosperity in other parts of the circuit, and now, that a two days' meeting was announced for Richmond, the attention of the people generally was turned in that direction. A Methodist two days' meeting was something new to most of the citizens, and created no little excitement; partly to know what it would be like, and, partly, because these "hireling preachers" were about to disturb the quiet of the place. Some were anxious to keep the people from attending, others, to see the great sight.

The meeting was held in the brick school-house, on the public square. When the time appointed arrived, the Methodists came in from different parts of the circuit. Mr. Beggs and two or three local preachers were in attendance. At the first coming together there was quite a congregation. An excellent sermon was preached, one that stirred the hearts of the people to their very depths, kindling anew the holy fire. At the close of the sermon the tide of feeling was running so high that the songs and shouts of the congregation were heard far away. This increased the excitement in the town. At night the school-house was crowded, the Holy Ghost attended the Word preached and the exhortation which followed. An invitation being given, five or six persons presented themselves as seekers of salvation. This was a strange sight to many in the house. The pious gathered around the penitents, singing and praying with them till a late hour.

On Sunday a love-feast was held. It was a time of power. Toward the close of the exercises, an invitation was given to persons to unite with the Church. Several came forward. Among the number were three sisters, Misses K., of one of the first families of the town. Their father was rather inclined to infidelity. He had taken great pains to educate and prepare his daughters to move in the highest circle of society, not dreaming they would ever be Methodists. When the three Misses K. came forward and united with the Church, some evil-designing one, on the outside of the house, who saw through the window what was going on within, hastened to Mr. K., and told him that the Methodists had got his daughters "befooled; that they were acting very disreputably, lying prostrate upon the floor," etc. This statement exasperated Mr. K. very highly. He immediately made his way to the school-house, where the love-feast was being held, and demanded admittance. The doorkeeper, not knowing what had been told him, refused to let him in. He forced open the door and entered, trembling with rage. Going to where his daughters sat weeping, he took them by the hand, and led them away. As they passed out, the exclamation, "Lord have mercy," in subdued tones, was heard from different parts of the congregation. When he reached his residence, his daughters informed him that all they had done was to unite with the Church. Finding that he had been deceived, that his informant had misrepresented his daughters and the Methodists, he led them back to the school-house and to the seat whence he had taken them. He then went to Rev. Mr. Beggs, and requested him to make an explanation of his course that morning, and offer an apology for him to the public congregation. He remained to hear the sermon, and, at the close of the services, invited the preachers to dine with him that day. He expressed an entire willingness, as it was the wish of his daughters, for them to be members of the Methodist Episcopal Church. They were soon after converted, and continued, at the last account from them, pious, influential members. Thus, Satan was thwarted in his design. This meeting resulted in much good. Preaching was continued in the school-house for some time, class and prayer meetings being held in a private house.

In the course of events it became necessary for the Methodists to leave that place of worship. Again they were without a tabernacle. The prospect looked gloomy. It was not long, however, till they found a place, not very inviting, it is true, in its appearance, but they were glad to find shelter any where. James Henry offered a small frame building which had been occupied as a residence. It was humble in its appearance, but was gladly accepted, and soon fitted up with rough seats and made as comfortable as the ability of the members would admit. Here the preachers again administered the Word of Life to the faithful few, and here prayer and class meetings were held, led by that good man, Elisha W. Fulton. Glorious seasons were enjoyed in this small tabernacle. The circuit preachers usually held class meeting immediately after preaching. If the sermon was a good one, and the preacher gave the members a class meeting after it, they went from their humble place of worship strong in the Lord. If the sermon was *not* so good, but the preacher held class meeting after preaching, all were well satisfied. Though the sermon was good, very good, if the preacher did *not* meet the class, the members went away feeling that they had had but half a loaf. If the sermon was a *poor* one, and the preacher did not meet the class, then the members returned to their homes sorry indeed. What was true of the little band in Richmond, at that time, in regard to desiring the preachers to meet the classes, was true with the members of the Church generally in the planting of Methodism in Indiana. In the use of this means of grace they grew in piety.

The house obtained from Mr. Henry was too small and too much out of repair to answer the purpose long. Something had to be done—some other arrangement made. The male members were called together for consultation. They were few in number—none rich—some very poor. After earnest prayer it was determined to build a house for the Lord. A subscription paper was prepared—all put down their names. A few men who were not members of the Church gave some aid. The largest amount given by any one was twenty-five dollars—the smallest, one dollar. One young man who was working for nine dollars per month, and boarding himself, gave ten dollars. A lot was purchased where the Pearl-Street Methodist Episcopal Church now stands, and the work commenced. The Church was to be one story in front, two in rear, being located on the side of a hill—the lower to be of stone, the upper frame. Though the men had subscribed all they thought they were able to give, they turned out, quarried the rock, drew them to the spot, dug out the foundations, and attended the masons while they built the wall and made it ready for the frame-work. They had not progressed far till the small amount raised by subscription was expended. There was no alternative left but to try it again. Accordingly, every man put down just half the amount of his first subscription. Again the work went on. When the house was up, inclosed, and the floors laid, the funds were again exhausted. Although compelled to cease operations for a time, the members were greatly rejoiced that they had some prospect of a house of worship of their own, from which they could not be driven by their enemies.

At this time Asa Beck and Richard S. Robinson were traveling the circuit. The members of the Church desired a two days' meeting in their new meeting-house. Mr. Robinson, the junior preacher, agreed to give them one. The time was fixed. Temporary seats and pulpit were arranged in the new church. Then most earnestly did the members of the Church pray that the Great Head of the

Church would meet them at their first two days' meeting in the new house of worship. At the prayer meetings and around the family altar this was the burden of their petitions. Arrangements were made with Rev. John A. Baughman, who was then traveling Greenville circuit, in Ohio, his family residing at Eaton, and whose fame as a preacher had reached Indiana, to attend this meeting. During all this time the opposition to Methodism had by no means abated in Richmond, and now that another two days' meeting was to be held, something *must* be done to prevent it. Accordingly, a report was put in circulation that "the small-pox was raging at Eaton," where Mr. Baughman resided, and as he was coming to the Methodist meeting it would not be safe to permit him to enter the town. Upon this report a committee, called a "Board of Health," was appointed. On Friday this "Board of Health" went to all the families whom it was supposed would be likely to entertain any Methodists that might come from a distance to attend the meeting that was to commence the next day, and warned them not to receive any company, "as the small-pox was then in Eaton," and the probability was, if Mr. Baughman came to the Methodist meeting, " that dreadful disease would spread among the citizens." They also appointed men to keep watch of the road leading from Eaton to Richmond, and prevent Mr. Baughman from entering the town.

The time for the meeting to commence arrived.

On Saturday morning the Methodists from the country met the few who lived in town, in the street in front of the new church. While they stood there sorrowing over the state of things surrounding them, they saw at some distance several groups of men watching them to see what they would do. The hour for the services to commence having arrived, Mr. Robinson, who was with them, said, "Well, friends, let us go into the house. I will preach, by the help of the Lord, if the devil stands at the door." They went in. The preacher gave out a hymn—they all joined in singing; after which they bowed before the Lord. Mr. Robinson prayed, and *such a prayer!* The power of God came down; the house trembled to its foundation; the souls of the pious caught new fire; their faith was increased and they felt that the Lord of Hosts was with them. The sermon which followed did their hearts good. At night there was preaching again—the congregation much increased. God was in their midst. Their battle-cry was, "The sword of the Lord and of Gideon!" The love-feast was held Sunday morning. It was a time long to be remembered. Truly,

"Their hearts did burn while Jesus spake,
 And glowed with sacred fire;
He stooped, and talked, and fed, and blessed,
 And filled the enlarged desire."

At the close of the love-feast, Mr. Baughman made his appearance among them. By affliction in his family he had been prevented from leaving Eaton on Saturday, as he had anticipated. Having heard nothing of the report put in circulation at Richmond, and the arrangements made to prevent him from entering the town, he left home at an early hour on Sunday morning, and before those who had been appointed to keep watch over the road were aware of it, he was among God's people at the church. The news that "Baughman was at the Methodist Church, and was going to preach," flew like lightning through the town. The people came in crowds. The leading infidels of the place, who had been active in getting up the opposition to the meeting, came. The house could not hold the people. Mr. Baughman took the pulpit, opened the services with singing and prayer, and then read for his text, Isaiah liii, 1: "Who hath believed our report, and to whom is the arm of the Lord revealed?" In his sermon, he took hold of the pillars of infidelity, and bore them off in triumph, and then razed the foundation thereof. Poor Infidelity! How pale and ghastly it appeared that day, under the mighty power of the truth! Mr. Baughman preached again at night. By this time, hearts were yielding; sinners were crying for mercy; the Lord was among his people in converting power, and the shouts of new-born souls were heard. The meeting closed on Monday. Thirty-two united with the Church, and about that number were converted. Among them was Rev. Silas Rawson, now of the

Indiana Conference. This meeting was a great victory for Methodism in Richmond. It was held in the Summer of 1831.

From that time the Methodist Episcopal Church has steadily advanced in that place. She had a hard struggle for a lodgment there. Sometimes her progress has been slow, and at other times more rapid. There are now two Methodist Churches, with large congregations, in that city. The little leaven, cast in that place by Rev. Russel Bigelow, still works.

CHAPTER XXIV.

STEADFASTNESS OF A PIOUS WIFE.

The Divine Being will always take care of those who trust in him, and unreservedly devote all their time and strength to his service. He will support, sustain, comfort, and deliver them in time of trouble.

In the year 1828, when Stephen R. Beggs traveled the Wayne circuit, Mrs. H. who then resided in Richmond, was deeply convicted for sin. She was awakened under a sermon preached by Mr. Beggs, from Psalm l, 14, 15: "Offer unto God thanksgiving, and pay thy vows unto the Most High, and call upon me in the day of trouble; I will deliver thee, and thou shalt glorify me." She had a long and hard struggle, but after weeks of deep penitency, found redemption in the blood of the Lamb; her burden of guilt was taken away, and her "mourning turned into joy." So intense was the agony of her mind before she found peace in believing, that she was almost incapable of attending to her domestic duties. So great was her joy when she felt that her sins were all forgiven, that she shouted aloud the praises of God, saying, "Now, Lord, from this time forth, in weal or in woe, in sickness or in health, in tribulation, distress, poverty, persecution, living or dying, I am thine—thine forever!" She connected herself with the Methodist Episcopal Church, casting in her lot with the little persecuted band in Richmond.

Her husband was a very wicked man, violently opposed to her piety, particularly to her being among the Methodists, who, on account of their religion, were not in the sweetest odor in the nostrils of most of the citizens of the town. He not only refused to render her any assistance, but by every means in his power strove to block up her way, prevent her from attending Church, and break her off from her piety, abusing the Methodists with oaths and curses, threatening her with violence if she did not desist from her religious course. He often crossed her in her domestic concerns, trying in every possible way to get her angry, thinking if he could only aggravate her to madness, the victory would be won, and his triumph complete; but in this he failed. While Mrs. H. was kind and affectionate, giving every necessary attention to the wants of her family, enduring the abuses heaped upon herself and the Methodists by her husband, never uttering an unkind word, or allowing a murmur to escape her lips, she did not allow his opposition or threats to deter her from the discharge of religious duties, but was faithful in all things, always at class and prayer meetings, and always in attendance upon the preaching of the Word. Her steadfastness con-

STEADFASTNESS OF A PIOUS WIFE. 179

tinued as time rolled along, though the opposition she met from her husband increased.

A two days' meeting was appointed in the country, a few miles from town. When the time drew near her husband forbade her going. She flew to the Lord, who was her "stronghold in the day of trouble." Receiving, as she believed, an answer that it was right for her to go, she made every arrangement she could for the comfort of her husband during her absence. When the time arrived she took her two children, and, being aided by some kind friends, made her way on Saturday to the place of the meeting, intending to return on Sunday evening. As the meeting progressed she was greatly blessed. While she spoke in the love-feast on Sunday morning, the Holy Ghost came down; every heart was thrilled, and every eye melted to tears. It rained throughout the day on Sunday, which raised Whitewater beyond fording, and Mrs. H. could not return to town that evening. The rain continued Sunday night, so that no one from the house where she had been staying could get to the church. There being several persons at the house where she was, they held a prayer meeting. During the exercises, Mrs. H. was called upon to pray. She poured out her burdened soul to God. Never did woman plead for a husband with greater earnestness.

During all this time her husband was at home, raging like a madman. When Sunday night came, and his wife did not return, he became furious. About midnight, concluding his wife had given herself to the Methodists, caring nothing for him, he resolved to burn up his house and all it contained "and run away by the light." He went to work and packed up his clothes. When all was ready, and he was about to kindle the fire to consume his house, it occurred to him that "it would be *too* cruel to burn the house and all its contents and leave his wife with the children, and nothing to help herself with." After a moment's pause he concluded to leave the house and goods for her, but "*he* would go and she should nevermore see his face." He took his pack and started, directing his steps toward Eaton, Ohio. When he had walked about four miles, suddenly the thought entered his mind, "This is just what my wife and the Methodists desire—to get rid of me." With an oath he determined they should not be gratified. "He would go back and devil them as long as he lived." Retracing his steps, when he reached town day was dawning. He went to his house—which he had left a little after midnight, intending never to return—and put away his clothes. His passion had been wrought up to such a pitch that he felt he *must* have revenge in some way. To this end he went to a liquor-saloon and took a potion, to nerve him more fully for his purpose. He then went out on the streets, intending to whip the first man that gave him a harsh word or an unpleasant look. To his utter discomfiture, every one he met was in a most pleasant humor. None gave him an unkind word. At this he was so chagrined he determined to commit suicide. But soon the thought occurred, "This is what my wife and the Methodists desire— any thing to get rid of me."

Toward noon of this day his wife returned home. As soon as she arrived he commenced cursing the Methodists, hoping thereby to provoke her to reply. He was again doomed to disappointment. In this he did not succeed, though he kept it up till a late hour at night. Finding this effort to provoke his wife into a dispute failed, he now tried another scheme—that was, to make her believe he would kill himself, hoping she would yield rather than "he should do that dreadful deed;" at least, that "she would try to dissuade him from his purpose." Mrs. H. did not make any reply, but with her heart uplifted to God in earnest prayer felt that he would overrule all for her good. Being defeated again, he did not know what to do.

In a few weeks after this, the first two days' meeting held in Richmond was to come off. When Mrs. H.'s husband heard that the meeting was appointed, he gave her most positive orders not to bring any Methodists about the house at that time. She gave no promise, but as the time drew near, made what preparation she could to accommodate a few friends. When the meeting came on, she invited two mothers in Israel home with her, on

Saturday. Her husband, finding they were at his house, would not go in till a late hour at night. On Sunday morning he ventured to the breakfast-table. While at the table the old ladies invited him to go with them to the love-feast that morning. Instantly he said within himself, "That's my chance! The Methodists have door-keepers when they hold love-feasts, and they talk to those who are not members of the Church before they let them in. I will go to the door, but will not go in. When I get there and they begin to talk to me, I will give the Methodists—preachers and people—a round cursing in the hearing of them all, and then turn away. That will be some gratification to me."

When the hour for love-feast arrived, he accompanied his wife and the two old ladies to the school-house where the meeting was held. As they drew near the door, there being quite a crowd there, he concluded to fall back a little till all had passed in, "lest the door-keeper might not speak to him, and then he would lose the opportunity of doing up that job of *cursing* he had prepared himself for." When they had all passed in he stepped upon the door-step. The door-keeper swung the door *wide* open. He stepped in and halted. The door-keeper, putting his arm around, drew him a little forward and closed the door without saying a word. Mr. H. turned pale, and trembling from head to feet, took a seat. The love-feast was a time of power. He had never been in one before—had not intended

STEADFASTNESS OF A PIOUS WIFE. 183

to be in this, "but was caught in a trap." He felt that his distress of mind was intolerable—that if the torments of the damned in hell were any greater than he had been enduring for months, he could not bear the thought. In that love-feast he resolved if there was any such religion as his wife and the Methodists professed he would have it or die seeking. From this time he sought the pardon of his numerous sins. The struggle continued for weeks. So great was his distress of mind that much of the time he could neither eat nor sleep. Now did Mrs. H. most devoutly pray that God would have mercy upon her husband. He was clearly and powerfully converted at a camp meeting, joined the Church and became as zealous in the cause of the Redeemer as he had been in that of Satan, and as ardently attached to the Church as he had been bitterly opposed to it. How wondrous the mercy of God! During all the time he was so fearfully opposing his wife in her pious course, the carnal mind was raging within him, fearful of being cast out. He was often heard to say, "The steadfastness of my pious wife, with God's blessing, saved me."

Had Mrs. H. yielded in the slightest degree, or faltered in her religious course, the probabilities are her husband never would have been converted, and she would have retrograded in her piety, if she had not entirely backslidden. The text from which the sermon was preached that was the instrument in her awakening, made a lasting impression upon her mind: "Offer unto God thanksgiving, and pay thy vows unto the Most High, and call upon me in the day of trouble; I will deliver thee, and thou shalt glorify me." To this she clung with great tenacity.

CHAPTER XXV.

REV. RUSSEL BIGELOW.

THE writer feels his inability to present such a sketch of Rev. Russel Bigelow as his great worth and eminent usefulness demand; nevertheless, as this distinguished servant of God spent two years of the prime of his ministerial life in Indiana, he offers this brief tribute. The facts respecting his early life are meager. From a sketch in one of the published volumes by Bishop Edward Thomson I find the following:

"Russel Bigelow was the third child, but eldest son, of respectable parents in the ordinary walks of life, both of whom survive him. He was born in Chesterfield, Cheshire, N. H., February 24, 1793. His opportunities for education were very limited, though he learned to read in early life, and in his very childhood was a diligent student of the Bible, and other religious books. When he was eight years old his father removed to Vermont. At the age of nine he was awakened and made a subject of converting grace under the preaching of the Methodist ministry, though he made no profession of religion at this time. Soon after his family removed to a parish in Lower Canada, where religious meetings were seldom held and religious persons rarely met with. He became a backslider in heart, and in this condition continued for four years. Under the earnest prayer of a sister, he was reclaimed, and found great peace in believing. He now—May, 1806—united with the society. Alluding to the repugnance which many feel to the reception of children into the Church, he often remarked, in later life, 'I expect to bless God eternally for the privilege of becoming a member while I was so young.' In his fifteenth year he felt that he *would* be called to preach. He continued to grow in grace, avoided the company of the thoughtless and gay, sought the society of the pious, and was derisively called by his young acquaintances 'the Deacon,' or 'the old Deacon.' In 1812 he removed to Worthington, O. About this time, when he was nineteen years of age, he was licensed to exhort. Unexpected trials and embarrassments awaited him in the pulpit, under the pressure of which he resolved to give up the idea of preaching. A horror now seized his mind, from which he could find no relief but in a quiet submission to his convictions of duty.

"He was industrious in his habits, and labored successfully with his hands; and though early urged to enter the itinerant ranks, he long delayed, being fearful lest he should 'run too fast.' His internal conflict was so great on one occasion that he 'wandered away.' Describing the feelings of his soul at this period, he says, 'I never came so near being willing to exchange situations with the reptiles of the earth as at this time.'

"On the 15th of October, 1814, having been admitted on trial in the Ohio Conference, he started for his first circuit, which was in Kentucky. His natural timidity, his youthful appearance, his low stature, his awkward manners, his unprepossessing face, and his slovenly dress, gave his congregations but poor promise of edification and instruction. Many a proud man sneered, and many a pious one prayed, as he entered the church with his saddle-bags in one hand and hat in the other, and bashfully hid himself in the pulpit. It was soon apparent that he was humble and devoted; and as he progressed in his discourse, the wicked lost their contempt, and the good their mortification; the sluggish were aroused, and the intelligent were amazed; arrows of conviction flew thick and fast; sinners were slain on the right and left; the atoning Lamb was lifted up, and the dead were made alive by his blood.

"His next circuit was Miami, on which he was associated with A. Cummins. In 1816, after having been ordained deacon, he was appointed to Lawrenceburg circuit, Indiana, where he was favored with the counsel of Allen Wiley, who was this year his beloved colleague. During this year he was married to Margaret Irwin, by whom he had seven children, who all survived him. In his journal he writes concerning his marriage these significant words, which the young would do well to ponder: 'I now think it would have been better had I remained single a few years longer.' His domestic embarrassments did not, however, diminish his domestic attachments."

Lawrenceburg was, at this time, 1817, the most important town in the State. Her citizens were intelligent. Among them were some of the most talented men of the West. The circuit was a laborious one to travel, covering a large scope of country. Mr. Bigelow labored on this circuit with great acceptability to the people. His talents, as a preacher, were much admired.

In 1823 he was sent to Whitewater circuit, with George Gatch for his colleague, which brought him back into the State. This was also a large circuit, embracing at that time all of what is now Franklin, Union, Wayne, and parts of Randolph, Henry, and Fayette counties. He located his family, for the year, in Centerville, the county seat of Wayne county, as it was the most central point in his circuit.

Mr. Bigelow was about medium hight, slender frame, and of feeble, physical constitution. His head was large for a man of his stature, forehead high, and very prominent. His piety was of the deepest character. No one doubted it. It manifested itself in his countenance, words, and actions. He exhibited, at all times, that he possessed "the spirit of Christ." Any one in his company would soon feel that he was in the presence of a man of God. And yet no one could form a proper estimate of his talents as a preacher, from his appearance. He was not what would generally be called a fine-looking man.

He was mighty in the Scriptures. He made them his daily study. The writer has heard him say, that he had "read the Bible through, several times, on his knees." He made it "the man of his counsel," and could have said, "I have hid thy law within my heart." He had a logical mind, and was a very close reasoner. He was a man of great humility—never exalted in his own estimation—much inclined to look upon his pulpit efforts as being feeble. Sometimes he felt much dejected after preaching, considering his efforts, "so poor, so inefficient in accomplishing good." On one occasion he preached a sermon on Saturday, at a quarterly meeting, which *he* thought was an exceedingly feeble *effort*. For sometime afterward he reproached himself bitterly for having made an entire failure— one "that accomplished no good." Three months after this, at the next quarterly meeting held in the same place, in the love-feast on Sunday morning, three young men arose in succession and professed to have obtained the pardon of their sins, stating that they had been awakened under the sermon preached by Mr. Bigelow, on Saturday, at the last quarterly meeting, and were thereby led to seek salvation. That was the sermon which Mr. Bigelow thought "had accomplished no good."

When he arose in the pulpit to open the services a stranger would not call him graceful, nor would expectation be very high. But soon it would be discovered that a man of master mind stood before the congregation.

Rev. J. B. Finley, in his *Autobiography*, gives the following account in regard to Mr. Bigelow. It occurred at Steubenville, Ohio, during the session of the Conference, held at that place. Mr. Finley being presiding elder of the district, was requested to assist in appointing the preachers to their places of lodging, during the session of the Conference. He says: "A request was handed to me by one of the stewards, from a gentleman of wealth, that if I would send him one of our most talented ministers, he would cheerfully keep him during the Conference. The gentleman was a member of the Episcopal Church, and had a worthy family, rather more than ordinarily refined, and enjoying all such elegancies of life as a country village would afford. Wishing to gratify him, I sent Russel Bigelow to be his guest. Now, Russel was dressed in plain, homespun apparel, cut and made with as much skill as home could furnish. It was not exactly that *à la mode* which suits fashionable life. The young Miss in the parlor cast many sidelong glances at the young preacher, who diffidently sat composing his features, and gazing at the various objects around him.

Meeting the steward, Mr. —— said, 'I do not think you have treated me right in sending me such a common, homespun-looking man.' At this the steward came to me in great haste, saying Mr. —— was displeased. 'Well,' said I, 'his request has been complied with; he asked for a talented man, and I have sent him the most talented man we have. Go and tell him that I wish him and his family to go to the Presbyterian Church to-morrow and hear him preach, and then if they are dissatisfied, I will remove him.'

"Sabbath came. The minister in homespun ascended the desk; all eyes were upon him. 'How finely he reads!' says ——. 'What distinct articulation!' said Mr. —— to his lady as they sat in the pew. 'Dear me,' said the daughter, 'how beautifully our country preacher reads poetry!' Then followed the prayer; and when, with warm heart, he prayed for the families who had, with generous hospitality, thrown open their houses for the entertainment of God's servants, the silent tear and half-suppressed sigh told of his power over the heart.

"He preached, and it was only as Russel Bigelow of sainted memory could preach. Indeed, it is said he excelled himself on that occasion. The effect upon the hearers was powerful, and upon none more so than upon his worthy host and family, who took him home, and sent for me to ask my pardon, remarking that he had never heard such a sermon in all his life."

Mr. Bigelow, from the time he read his text to the close of his sermon, would remind you of the most skillful master-mechanic from the time that mechanic made the first mark upon the timber with his square and compass, through all the operation, till the superstructure was reared up complete in every part, each piece of timber fitting exactly in its place, the whole, when completed, presenting the most beautiful specimen of architectural skill. Few men, if any, excelled him in analyzing a subject. He exhibited all its parts, and then brought all together in one complete whole. His sermons presented the most beautiful symmetry—perfect in every part. As he advanced in his discourse, the inspiration increased, his voice rising and swelling, his countenance glowing with increasing luster as he became more and more absorbed in his subject, till he seemed to be lost to every thing else. He would hold his congregation as if spell-bound, carrying his hearers with him, till they, too, like himself, lost sight of every thing but the subject he was unfolding before them.

His eloquence was peculiar to himself—difficult to describe. No one can form a correct idea of his overwhelming pulpit power who never heard him. In 1823, when he traveled Whitewater circuit, he was requested to preach a sermon in Centerville on the fourth day of July, which he consented to do. The word went out through all the country round about. When the day arrived the people came in from six and eight miles. The congregation was large, men of the legal and medical professions being generally present. When the hour for the services to commence arrived, after the opening prayer Mr. Bigelow read for his text, "He hath not dealt so with any nation." Psalm cxlvii, 20. We can not attempt at this distant period to give a description of the sermon further than to say that its effect on the audience was overwhelming, making an impression upon the hearts and minds of many who heard it that time can never erase. It was, perhaps, the greatest sermon of his life. All went away impressed as they never had been before with the great truth that "the Lord reigneth" among the nations of the earth. In the forty-third year of his age, on July 1, 1835, in the city of Columbus, Ohio, this holy man of God passed away from earth to heaven. The Church felt deeply his loss, for he was greatly beloved. I can but quote again the words of Bishop Thomson:

"Russel Bigelow had the manners of a gentleman, the graces of a Christian, and the gifts of an orator. His favorite theme was the atonement. This gave animation to his hopes, fire to his tongue, luster to his discourses, harmony to his doctrines, and efficacy to his labors. On all the cardinal doctrines of the Gospel he was clear and uncompromising, eliminating them from error with a hand that never wanted cunning, and heart that never wanted courage. His favorite book was the Bible, which he was accustomed to study through and through, by course, upon his knees.

"His favorite refreshment was prayer. To this he devoted the first moments after he rose from his bed. At eight o'clock he retired again for closet devotion. For the last five years of his life, however, in order that he might be at the throne of grace at the same time that a beloved brother—Rev. Mr. S.—was there, he changed the hour to nine o'clock. At midday he sought again the Sun of Righteousness; three o'clock, and twilight, and the hour before retiring to rest, were other periods when he devoutly and privately communed with God. Thus, morning, noon, and night—at nine, at three, and at twilight, did this good man regularly retire to his 'closet.' The hour which he most prized was twilight, because it was associated with his regeneration. At this time he was accustomed to remember every preacher on his district, and every awakened person who had within the last three months solicited an interest in his prayers. He would bring them, name by name, before God, dwelling upon the peculiar dangers, or trials, or wants of each case as a father would plead for his children.

"His family prayers were marked by all the fervor and energy of his more public ministration. Indeed, *earnestness* marked all his labors. Whether in private or public, teaching in the Sabbath school, praying at the altar, preaching on the camp-ground, presiding in the Conference, or writing in the committee-room, he was a man of zeal. Love animated and sustained him; so that his zeal was tempered with sweetness, his firmness with mildness, his courage with tenderness, and his godly daring with a most subduing affection, as if, like his Master, he would 'draw all men unto him.' *Just* to conscientiousness, *exact* to scrupulousness, and orderly as a field-marshal, he avoided even the *appearance* of evil.

"Long-suffering and forbearing, his expostulations with sinners were in tones of mercy, till mercy ceased to be a virtue, when he rose with the majesty of a monarch to assert the dignity of law in tones that made the rebellious tremble. This, however, was not often the case. His charity covered a multitude of sins. It was ingenious perhaps to a fault, in devising excuses for offenders, and putting the most favorable aspects upon every case.

"At the root of all his excellencies was a mighty *faith.* He believed God implicitly; relied upon him unwaveringly; wrestled with him victoriously; continuing in prayer till petition burst into thanksgiving."

CHAPTER XXVI.

REV. ALLEN WILEY.

The subject of this sketch was among the first, if not *the* first man licensed to preach by a quarterly conference of the Methodist Episcopal Church in the State of Indiana. Nearly all his Christian and ministerial life being spent in Indiana, he deserves a place in every record of the rise and progress of Methodism in the State.

"The Life and Times of Rev. Allen Wiley, by Rev. F. C. Holliday," has been given to the Church and the world. Though in that volume a more extended notice of the life and labors of Mr. Wiley is given, the writer, having known him from early boyhood, would bear some humble testimony to his worth.

Allen Wiley was born in Frederick county, Virginia, 1789. When he was some nine years old his father emigrated to the State of Kentucky. In the Fall of 1804 his father removed to the Territory of Indiana and settled in the Whitewater country, not far from where the town of Harrison now stands. Here he grew up to manhood and married a wife. He was awakened to the subject of salvation in family prayer, led by a brother of his wife.

In 1810, in the twenty-second year of his age, under the ministry of Rev. Moses Crume, he united with the Methodist Episcopal Church and was converted in a love-feast meeting a few months afterward. It was not long after that he was licensed to exhort, for it was soon discovered that he had talents for great usefulness if they were cultivated. July, 1813, he was licensed to preach.

In December, 1816, he was employed by the presiding elder to travel Lawrenceburg circuit with Rev. Russel Bigelow, who was in charge. This circuit embraced the neighborhood where Mr. Wiley resided. Here, where he had reached his manhood, where he had married, and where he had his home, he commenced his itinerant labors. At the close of this Conference year, in the Summer of 1817, he was admitted on trial into the Ohio Annual Conference. Having labored with so much acceptability to the people on Lawrenceburg circuit, he was appointed to that circuit as junior preacher, with Samuel West as preacher in charge. In those days it was a rare thing to put a man in charge the first year he was admitted into the traveling connection. They were generally placed as junior preachers, with some man of experience in charge, to teach them how to do the work of an itinerant preacher; how to meet the classes, hold prayer meetings, visit the families, and administer the Discipline of the Church.

Mr. Wiley traveled large and laborious circuits

for several years, which subjected him to great toil, exposure, and privation. He served the Church many years as presiding elder, and filled the most important stations in Indiana. His last appointment was to Centenary station, New Albany.

His early opportunities for securing an education were not good, his early boyhood and youth, from the time he was about nine years of age, being spent in the backwoods of Kentucky and in the wilds of Indiana. Up to manhood, though his thirst for knowledge was great, he had not been able to do more than learn to read and write, and study common arithmetic. Colleges and high schools were not in the country, and his father did not possess the means to send him to the old States to go to school. After his conversion, and particularly after he was licensed to preach, his thirst for an education was greatly increased; and though he had commenced opening a farm in the dense forest, with a young and increasing family around him, he determined to cultivate his mind and increase his information in science and literature. He procured what books he could, and commenced anew his studies without a teacher. Having his land to clear, fence, and cultivate, in order to procure sustenance for his family, he had no time to devote to study except during the hours of early morn, and the night after he had finished his daily toil, and during those intervals when it was necessary to take some relaxation from labor. His rule was to carry his book with him, and when he found it necessary to sit down a moment to rest, he would take it up and apply his mind with all the energy he possessed. In this way he spent something more than two years, not allowing one moment to run to waste, taking no more time for sleep than was absolutely necessary. In the course of one Spring and Summer he cleared several acres of ground, made the rails and fenced it, and cultivated his fields, and studied the English grammar thoroughly.

After he entered the itinerancy he pursued his studies with increased energy. The circuits being large, and having as a general thing to preach every day through the week and twice on the Sabbath, besides meeting the classes, with much traveling to do between his appointments, he had no time for study, except when riding on horseback, or at night, and in the morning before he started on his way. These opportunities he improved to the best advantage. In this way, while traveling circuits and districts, without an instructor, he acquired a knowledge of the Latin, the Greek, and Hebrew languages. There were few, if any, better Latin, Greek, or Hebrew scholars in the West than Mr. Wiley. On one occasion, while he was presiding elder, he met, by invitation, several ladies and gentlemen in a social circle. Among the number present was a young M. D. who had just entered upon his profession. He, knowing that Mr. Wiley was a Greek scholar, was very loquacious on the subject of Greek literature, professing to be an adept himself. The conversation had not proceeded far till Mr. Wiley was impressed that this young M. D.'s knowledge of Greek was very superficial. He determined to test him. Accordingly, he drew from his pocket a Greek Testament, and, handing it to the doctor, requested him to read a portion and give his translation of it. Perceiving the doctor was much embarrassed, Mr. Wiley requested him to read a particular text. The young M. D., with increased embarrassment, remarked that "he was, indeed, very rusty in Greek," and asked to be excused. Mr. Wiley excused him, and there the conversation ended on the subject of the Greek classics.

Mr. Wiley had a most cordial dislike to a pedant—to one who professed to be more learned than he really was. His ambition was to be thorough in every study he commenced, and not allow himself to be superficial in any thing. Of every subject he took hold he endeavored to search it to the bottom. Theology was his main study. In that he took great and constant delight. All his other studies were for the purpose of aiding him in his theological studies. He was a profound theologian.

If universities and colleges had been as lavish in conferring the degrees of A. M. and D. D. in the days of Mr. Wiley as now, he would doubtless have received both the degrees, for no man in Indiana was more worthy.

He was of medium hight, agile, with a well-set

physical frame, walked erect, with quick step, and to the end of his life eschewed the use of a walking-cane. It was a source of much annoyance to him to see young ministers, in the full vigor of manhood, carrying a walking-stick.

His hair was dark, and quite thin on his head. In his latter years he became bald. His head was small, but well proportioned, with a finely-developed forehead. His mouth was finely curved, a dimple in his chin, his complexion fair, and when pleased he wore a very prepossessing smile. Perhaps he was never known to laugh aloud during the whole course of his ministerial life.

His countenance, when in the pulpit, was solemn, showing to all who looked upon him that he had a sense of the Divine presence, and felt that to God he should give an account for every word he uttered. He never while preaching allowed himself to say a light or foolish thing. It has often been remarked that the solemn countenance and manner of Allen Wiley in the pulpit made a deeper impression for good than the *sermons* of some ministers.

His voice was pleasant when in conversation, and was not unpleasant when he was preaching, though it was somewhat monotonous—sometimes rather heavy. There were inflections, but they were usually the same, rising to a certain pitch and continuing for a sentence or two, then falling to a lower key. In his tones, however, there was something peculiarly solemn.

As a pastor he was most indefatigable—faithfully visiting all the members of his flock, paying special attention to the sick, aged, and poor. He was punctual in filling all his engagements—seldom behind the hour to fill a private appointment, or meet a public congregation. He never allowed himself to be "behind the time." He was for many years one of the leading men of the Indiana Conference, always taking great interest and an active part in all the business of the Conference, always in his place, usually occupying the same seat during the entire session. It seldom, if ever, occurred that Allen Wiley was out of his place and had to be sent for when any thing was before the Conference in connection with which he was needed.

As a preacher he was systematic in the arrangement of his sermons. He was an expounder of the Holy Scriptures. He never indulged in fancy, nor made an effort to embellish his discourses—seldom relating an anecdote. He did not so much *charm* his hearers as he *impressed* them with a sense of the importance of his subject, fixing the text firmly in the mind. His utterances were distinct. He always spoke with earnestness, exhibiting that he felt fully all he said, and that the truths he was presenting were vital to the salvation of souls. No one ever thought that Allen Wiley preached merely to fill his appointment, or to make a display of his knowledge.

In 1818, when he traveled the Whitewater circuit, he held a two days' meeting in Salisbury, which was then the county seat of Wayne. The services were held in the court house, commencing on Saturday. Mr. Wiley being a great favorite with the people they came in from all the surrounding country, some a distance of twenty miles. He preached an impressive sermon Saturday. On Sunday, when the hour for preaching arrived, the court-house was crowded to its utmost capacity. Mr. Wiley came in, walked up to the judge's bench, and kneeled a short time in silent prayer. When he arose, on turning round, facing the audience, he discovered upon the hand-board the following note: "Preach from this text to-day and I will hear you: 'And God said unto Moses, I AM THAT I AM; and he said, Thus shalt thou say unto the children of Israel, I AM hath sent me unto you.'" Exodus iii, 14. He stood for a moment, the audience perceiving that something was moving his soul. He again kneeled down and remained some time in silent prayer. When he arose he announced his hymn; the congregation joined in singing; after which he made the opening prayer. In that prayer most earnestly did he plead for Divine help while he should that day stand as an "embassador for Christ," and that the Holy Spirit might carry the Word with power to the heart of some one in the congregation unknown to him, yet known to God.

Divine power rested upon the audience while

he was praying. Many hearts were touched. After prayer he read the note he had found upon the hand-board, then opened his Bible and announced his text, as requested. For about the space of two hours he unfolded the text with a pathos and power that told upon the congregation. In those days Arianism was rife in that region, but on this occasion it received a blow from which it never recovered. Many who heard that sermon, and continued to hear Mr. Wiley for many years afterward, considered it the great sermon of his life. He was often, afterward, heard to say that he had never, on any other occasion, felt so sensibly "the power of Christ resting upon him." It was ascertained that the note was written by a young lawyer whose name was Dally. He soon after that left the country and went to New Orleans.

Mr. Wiley was considered one of the ablest preachers of the West, and will be remembered as long as those live who had the privilege of hearing him. Eleven years he traveled laborious circuits, five years he was stationed in the most important towns in Indiana, fourteen years he faithfully discharged the duties of presiding elder. He was elected delegate to the General Conference four times in succession. He served one term as a member of the Western Book Committee at Cincinnati, and was for several years one of the Trustees of Indiana Asbury University. He died in Vevay, Indiana, July 23, 1848. His death was caused by an injury which he received while performing some manual labor about the premises of a new residence he was preparing. His injury was not thought at first to be serious, but in a short time it proved fatal. When the fact was made known to him it did not alarm him. He immediately arranged all his temporal affairs, and on the holy Sabbath he quietly fell asleep in Jesus, in the fifty-ninth year of his age, and the thirty-fifth of his ministry.

CHAPTER XXVII.

REV. NEHEMIAH B. GRIFFITH.

Mr. Griffith was born in Whitehall, Washington county, New York, 1798. In the eighteenth year of his age, with his father's family, he emigrated to the State of Ohio. His surroundings in youth were such as led him into the gayest and most fashionable circles of society. Being of ready wit, of active mind, and lively temperament, he was charmed by the giddy mazes of the dance, and became exceedingly fond of the terpsichorean art. He was a great favorite in the circle in which he moved. After he became pious he greatly lamented the follies of his youth, and bore constant testimony to the pernicious influences of the ball-room.

When about twenty-one years of age, through the instrumentality of Rev. William H. Raper, he was awakened, converted, and brought into the Methodist Episcopal Church. In a few months afterward, he received the blessing of entire sanctification. From this time to the close of his life he was wholly consecrated to the Lord. His talents, piety, and zeal were such, that the Church soon licensed him to preach, and in the Fall of 1822 he was admitted on trial into the Ohio Conference.

All his itinerant life, except one year, was spent

in Indiana. His first field of labor was Madison circuit, as junior preacher. His second, Wilmington circuit, in Ohio. Here he was in charge and alone. His third appointment was to Whitewater circuit as junior preacher. This brought him back into Indiana. His fourth field of labor was Connersville circuit, where he was in charge with a colleague. His fifth appointment was to Rushville, where he labored alone. His sixth was to Indianapolis, alone. His seventh was to Lawrenceburg, with E. G. Wood for a colleague. His eighth returned him in charge of Lawrenceburg circuit, with R. S. Robinson for a colleague.

In the Fall of 1830 he was sent as the first missionary to Fort Wayne. This place was remote from any other field of labor. It was connected with the Madison district, and the presiding elder, Rev. Allen Wiley, in visiting Fort Wayne this year to hold a quarterly meeting, had to travel through a wilderness of some thirty miles, which was inhabited by Indians. This was a hard field for Mr. Griffith to cultivate, subjecting him to many perils and privations.

In the Fall of 1831 he was sent to South Bend mission. Again he was called upon to break up new ground. That portion of Indiana was then being rapidly settled. The people generally lived in log-cabins. Mr. Griffith, being the first itinerant preacher sent among them, he had to form his circuit and do all his preaching in the cabins of the settlers.

In the Fall of 1832 he was sent to Lafayette, with Richard Hargrave for his colleague. The next year he was returned to Lafayette, with H. Vredenburg as junior preacher. This was his last field of labor. Here he closed up his itinerancy, and was transferred to the New Jerusalem above, not to preach, but to join in the song of the redeemed, and swell louder the anthem of praise, "Unto Him that loved us, and hath washed us from our sins in his own blood."

On the twenty-second day of August, 1834, at his father's house in St. Joseph county, Indiana, he died in holy triumph, shouting with his expiring breath, "Glory! glory! glory! sweet heaven! I am coming!" Thus passed away one of the most deeply-pious and zealous ministers of the Lord Jesus that ever labored in Indiana. Mr. Griffith was a close student, and made great proficiency in his theological studies. He dearly loved the doctrine and Discipline of the Methodist Episcopal Church. He devoted all his energies, physical and mental, to the cause of his Master. He made no compromise with sin—never allowing any one to transgress the Divine law in his presence unreproved. If, in the day of judgment, there are any ministers whose skirts are found clear of the blood of souls, *Nehemiah B. Griffith* will be among them.

In 1829, when traveling the Lawrenceburg circuit, as he was on his way to his appointment one Sabbath morning, he saw a young man fishing in Hogan.

Mr. Griffith turned aside to where he was and faithfully reproved him, warning him of the consequences of Sabbath desecration, and tenderly and kindly invited him to lay aside his fishing-rod and go with him to the house of worship and give his heart to God. The young man declined, saying he would risk the consequences. Mr. Griffith left him and rode on to his appointment with a sad heart, feeling that the judgments of the Almighty might soon overtake him. Before nine o'clock the next morning that young man's soul was in the eternal world. He undertook to drive a span of fractious, fiery horses in the town of Lawrenceburg. They ran off with the vehicle and threw him against the curb-stone, dashing out his brains, and killing him instantly. Mr. Griffith gave him the last warning he ever received, improving the last opportunity to do so.

Mr. Griffith had a pleasant voice, and was a fluent speaker. His sermons were well arranged, logical, and seldom failed to make a deep impression upon those who heard them. He had great power with God in prayer. Revival influence attended his labors wherever he went. He brought many souls to Christ, and will have many stars in the crown of his rejoicing. He was a holy man of God—a burning, and shining light. His sun went down in the meridian of life, but it sat in a clear sky. Servant of God! though years have passed away since thy voice was hushed in death, thou art still remembered in Indiana!

CHAPTER XXVIII.

THE YOUNG LAWYER.

J. H. was born in one of the eastern counties of Indiana when the country was new. During his early boyhood the sources of information and opportunities for cultivating his mind were very limited. These being used to the best advantage he soon learned to read, and exhibited quite a fondness for books. As he advanced toward manhood, and his intellect began to be developed, he occasionally had thoughts of future greatness. He had a fondness for disputation, and evinced considerable skill in managing a controversy with his juvenile associates. By close application and the improvement of the opportunities afforded him, as well as he could, by the time of his arrival at manhood, he had acquired, for those days, a fair English education. After some deliberation as to his course in life he determined to devote himself to the study and profession of the law. Accordingly some law-books were procured, a preceptor engaged, and young H. entered upon the study of the law. Devoting all his energies to his studies he made rapid progress, and was, as soon as could reasonably have been expected, licensed to practice and admitted to the bar.

His thoughts now turned upon where he could locate himself and enter upon his profession. He placed what few articles of apparel he possessed in a knapsack, took that upon his back and set out on foot in search of a location. Directing his steps westward he, after several days' travel, late in the afternoon arrived at the town of N. and took lodgings at the hotel. N. was the county seat of H. county, and was situated on one of the finest rivers in Indiana. The town had but few inhabitants, the county having just been organized. When morning came he went forth to reconnoiter the place and to see what the prospect was. After spending most of the day in surveying the town, and in conversation with the citizens as to the prospects of their new county, he concluded to make an effort to establish himself there as a lawyer. His appearance did not impress the people very favorably as to his *legal ability*. His garments were of rough texture and much worn; he had come to the place a pedestrian, not on horseback nor in a coach. "He does not *look* much like a lawyer," the people said. Mr. H. discovered that the citizens were indisposed to recognize him as an "Attorney." He knew his appearance was not showy, that he was poor and among strangers. Feeling that his success in his profession depended upon his energy and faithfulness to business, he determined not to yield to the discouragements that surrounded him. After having made considerable effort he succeeded in obtaining a room for an office. It was necessary to save what little money he had to pay his board, and therefore he could not spend much in furnishing his office. A rough writing-table and one chair constituted his office furniture. One copy of the "Statute Laws of Indiana" constituted his library.

Thus equipped our young lawyer started off in his profession. It was not very long till a case of litigation occurred before a justice of the peace. He was employed as attorney for one of the parties. Though in the management of this case he did not show himself to be very learned in the law, he displayed such tact and skill as to attract the attention of all who attended the trial. When the case was decided it was in favor of Mr. H.'s client, notwithstanding the counsel for the opposite party was considered able. Having gained his cause in this, his *debut*, his way was open, and the people began to recognize him as a lawyer. In the course of a few months he was pretty well established in the practice of law. He enlarged his library as rapidly as he could procure means. He was a close student, and gave his undivided attention to every case in which he was employed. In the course of twelve months he had quite an extensive practice.

Unfortunately for Mr. H. his parents were not religious. His moral training had *all* been wrong. He had been taught to look upon Christianity with disdain, and upon all who made its profession with distrust. Thus, in early life, his mind received a strong bias against every thing like piety. When about eighteen years of age his attention was called to the system of Universalism. The fundamental principle of this system, that "all men will be holy and happy in a future state," delighted him. He commenced reading the Scriptures in order to fortify himself so as to defend *that* doctrine. He had not continued this course of reading long till he was convinced that the system was not taught in the Bible—that the Bible clearly taught the doctrine of man's accountability to his Maker; that it also taught a future general judgment, and the future punishment of the finally impenitent. There was now no alternative left but to embrace "orthodoxy" or renounce the *Bible* as a revelation from God, and espouse infidelity. He chose the latter. From the time he made this choice he boldly avowed himself an infidel.

Being naturally fond of controversy, and his profession leading him into constant debate, in all his leisure hours he sought opportunities to get into a dispute with some one on his favorite, "Infidelity *versus* Christianity." He delighted greatly in confounding those who entered into an argument with him. Persons who were not well posted in the Scriptures or in logic could not meet his sophistries or correct his misquotations from the Old and New Testaments, for he, like Voltaire and other infidels, made his quotations from the writings of infidels instead of the Bible; hence they were seldom correct. He was bold in declaring the "Bible to be the production of priestcraft, the religion of the Lord Jesus a cunningly-devised fable, and that Christianity would do for weak-minded men and women; but strong-minded, intellectual persons could not be beguiled into its support."

He was so outspoken in his infidelity that his society was shunned by many Christians; but the wicked gathered around him, and some of them were delighted to hear him denounce the Bible, and Christianity, and piety. His success in his profession was such as to bring a large amount of business into his hands, and he bade fair to take a high position as a lawyer.

The population of the town and country rapidly increased. Some families that came in were from the New England States. Among those latter was a Mr. E., whose wife's sister, Miss A., accompanied them. She had been pretty well educated, but was not pious; she was handsome, proud, of cheerful spirits, and quite attractive. She had not been long in the place till Mr. H. was charmed by her appearance. He sought an opportunity to make her acquaintance. Their acquaintance ripened into attachment, and after a few months they were united at Hymen's altar. Their union seemed to be a happy one, and Mr. H. prosecuted his profession with increased energy.

About one year after his marriage a Methodist

THE YOUNG LAWYER. 215

camp meeting was held a few miles from N. For some reason Mr. H. attended, a thing very uncommon for him, as he seldom visited the place of worship. While at the camp meeting he was observed to give special attention to the services. This was still further astonishing to those who knew him, and caused various conjectures as to what were his motives. None had known him to treat religious worship with so much respect. After the close of this camp meeting he frequently attended the Thursday night prayer meetings in town, always taking a seat in the rear of the congregation near the door. About the close of the prayer meeting he would retire, apparently desiring to be unnoticed. This unusual course was observed, and caused remark and anxiety. Some thought his object was to obtain something of which he could make sport in his attacks upon Christianity, but no one ventured to question him on the subject. He continued thus to attend the prayer meetings for some considerable length of time.

After months had passed, Mr. H. was called to a neighboring village on professional business. The suit in which he was engaged was one of great interest to the parties. Able counsel had been employed on the opposite side. The contest was a severe one, and great forensic skill was displayed by the attorneys on both sides. Mr. H. became much enlisted and put forth his best effort, exhausting much of his physical strength.

For some time an insidious disease had been lurking in his system, though unknown to himself or his friends, and by the close of the trial he was taken violently ill. He returned home about nightfall, very sick, and took his bed to rise no more. A physician was immediately summoned who exercised all his medical skill, but to no avail. The next day he was much worse and seemed to be rapidly sinking into the arms of death. Several of the citizens called to see him. Among them was Mr. S., a Methodist class-leader. After all had retired or were retiring, save those who were nursing, Mr. H. fixed his eyes upon Mr. S. as he, too, was leaving, and with a look expressive of the most *intense* anxiety and emotion said, "Mr. S., call again *soon*." Mr. S., promising compliance, left the room under a strong impression that the last moments of Mr. H. were near; that his sun of life was fast declining; that a few more hours, or days at most, would end his earthly career, and the realities of eternity would reveal his system of infidelity to be false, *woefully false*—pondering, too, in his own mind what that look, so expressive, which seemed to say there was a world of commotion within; that some powerful passions or principles were contending for the mastery, he could but inquire what it all meant; whether it could be possible his infidelity, upon which he had seemed to rely with so much confidence, was now failing him.

As Mr. S. walked slowly to his residence, ruminating upon the past, and contemplating the future, he breathed an earnest prayer to God that he would open the eyes of Mr. H., that he might, ere he left the world, renounce his infidelity.

After remaining at home for a short time, Mr. S. returned to the house of Mr. H. When he entered there were no persons present but a neighboring lady and Mrs. H., whose countenance plainly told the deep sorrow of her heart and her fearful apprehension that a dark cloud was gathering over her that would soon break in overwhelming trouble. The night before her husband was taken ill she had been greatly disturbed in her slumber. She saw, in her sleep, "a lady clad in a long, flowing robe of black approaching the gate"—which was a little way in front of their house—"seated upon a white horse, richly caparisoned, leading by her side a black horse with his equipage all hung in mourning. When she reached the front fence she alighted, fastened the steeds, and passing over the stile, came into the house. Addressing Mr. H. she informed him she had a summons for him—that he must go with her immediately. She told him to bid his wife and infant son farewell, for he would see them no more. Mr. H. begged for time to make preparations, stating that 'he was not prepared to meet such a summons.' The lady informed him that the summons would admit of no delay—that he had long since been warned that it *would* come, and that as he knew not the time, he should have made the necessary preparation, and should have held himself in readiness. Mr. H., with great earnestness, besought her to grant him but a short time to prepare. Her answer was '*No.*' He then refused to go. She with stern voice bade him follow her. He said 'he would not.' She took him by the arm and led him out of the house, he constantly saying, 'I can not go; I will not go.' When they reached the stile he attempted to get upon the *white* horse. The lady forbade him, commanding him to get upon the *black* horse. He obeyed. The lady seated herself upon the white horse, and, leading the way, Mr. H. following, uttering the most mournful lamentations, they soon disappeared in the distance."

This vision affected Mrs. H. so much that she awoke from her sleep. So clear was the whole scene to her view, and so deep the impression made upon her mind, she slept no more that night. Dreadfully apprehensive that some sore trial awaited her, and fearing that it would disturb Mr. H., she did not inform him of the vision she had seen. And now that he was *so ill*, fast sinking into death's cold embrace, her vision stood before her as an *awful* reality. She had no hope of her husband's recovery.

Mr. S. having entered the room, Mr. H. beckoned him to his bedside and attempted to speak, but his heart was too full, his voice faltered, his tongue failed to articulate. Struggling to get the mastery of his feelings he made a second effort. Addressing Mr. S. he said, "Sir, death has come to summon me from time to eternity; how can I go?" Raising both his hands, with a steady upward gaze, he exclaimed, "O, if"—his voice again failing—"if, if it did not seem so inconsistent—and I had almost rather die than be inconsistent—I would want you to pray for me." Mr. S. said, "If that is your desire it shall be granted. I trust there is mercy for you." "Do you think so?" he anxiously inquired. Mr. S. answered, "Yes, I trust there is." "Then *do, do* pray for me!" There being some moments of delay in order that the two ladies present might join in prayer, he said, "Do not wait one moment; pray *now*. There is no time for delay. I must soon be gone. I shall soon be in eternity. The messenger is already here. Get right down upon your knees and pray for me." The two ladies and Mr. S. bowed at the bedside while he endeavored to pray. His feelings were so wrought upon by what was transpiring that it was difficult for him to utter a word. Here was a dying man, one who had boasted of his infidelity and ridiculed religion, denouncing the "Bible as a forgery, a bundle of lies," now that he was on the very threshold of eternity desiring to be prayed for; by one, too, he had so often tried to confound on the subject of man's accountability to God, the reality of a future state of being, and the necessity of a preparation for death. While prayer was being offered the feelings of Mr. H. became so excited, and the agony of his mind so great that he cried aloud for mercy till much exhausted. The screams of the two ladies, mingled with his cries and the voice of prayer, brought several persons to the door, for it was considered exceedingly strange that prayer should be heard in the house of this infidel lawyer. After the close of the prayer, when all had become a little composed, Mr. H. said to Mr. S.: "Now, if you will raise me up and sit behind me I will try to talk a little before I die." His request was complied with. He commenced by saying, "You know I have been an avowed infidel. You know I have poured contempt upon Christianity—declared the Bible to be the production of priestcraft; but O, how sadly I have been mistaken! How astonishing it is that I never saw myself before! Often have I listened while death-bells were tolling; often have I looked upon the funeral procession, moving with slow and measured steps to the tomb. Yes, I have again and again stood upon the verge of the grave, beheld the coffin lowered to its cold, damp vault, and heard the deep-drawn sigh and mournful cry of those whose hearts had been smitten by grief; and yet for myself, O thoughtless man that I have been, for myself I never took one serious thought. And now, here I am, racked by pain, borne rapidly down by disease, sinking fast into a gaping grave. My principles have failed me. I find my infidelity will not sustain me, now that I am dying. O, what *shall* I do? How *can* I die? *Must* I go? Is there *no* delay? Can I have *no* time to prepare?" After a short pause he continued: "How inconsistent this seems in me, when I have so long denounced every thing like religion; but I can not help it. *Soon* I shall be beyond the boundaries of time, and must *now* be honest."

Addressing himself particularly to Mr. S. he said, "I thought some of uniting myself with your Church at your last camp meeting, but feared some would say I did it to gain professional business, and I deferred it. Now I must soon *die;* I must *go* without being prepared. Tell all your people, all the members of the Church, I want them to pray for me."

By this time a number of persons had gathered into the room, having heard the screams of Mrs. H., for she was now almost frantic with grief. Many of the expressions her husband had just uttered were *precisely* the same she had heard him make in the vision she saw two nights before. Among those who had just come into the room was a lady, who, hearing Mr. H.'s remarks, said to him, "You must be still; you must not talk so; you are injuring yourself; you are not going to die; you must lie down and keep composed." To this he replied: "Then lay me down and let me die."

At the request of Mr. H., Mr. S. remained with him, he and Mr. M. nursing him "till life's last hour had fled." He continued to grow worse the remainder of that day, the following night, and the next day. Though several physicians had been in attendance, the disease baffled their skill. Mr. H. steadily sank.

As he tossed himself upon his bed, from hour to hour, he would exclaim, "O, God! I can not die! I will not die! I must not go!" then he would call upon his two attendants for help, begging them to not let him die. Truly, "the frantic soul raved round the walls of its clay tenement—ran to each avenue and shrieked for help, but shrieked in vain." He was not permitted to enjoy one moment composed, but,

"Like a reptile on a bed of embers,
Turning, he languished;"

pleading to be placed first in one position and then in another.

About midnight, the third night of his illness, he requested Mr. S. to go out and get upon his front stile and cry at the top of his voice, "O, yes! O, yes! O, yes! J. H. is dying," and repeat it three times. When told that the people were asleep, and that it would disturb them, he replied, "That is the reason why I want you to do it. *They* are asleep—*I* am dying, and *they* don't know it. Do, do, Mr. S., grant a poor dying man this last request."

He would not be satisfied till Mr. S. retired, as if to comply with his request. About the dawn of day, he threw his arms around the neck of Mr. S. as he leaned over the bed, and expired. Among his last words were, "Must I die? Is there no help?"

When it was discovered that the taper of life had

burned out, his young wife, who was standing by his bed, fell backward, screaming, "He's gone! he's gone! He was my god! and the only god I worshiped!" No wonder her heart was now riven, and she was overwhelmed with anguish, when her *god*, the "*only* god she worshiped," had expired.

In the afternoon of the next day, the lifeless remains of Mr. H. were followed by a large concourse of people to the grave, which had been prepared on the bank of the beautiful river that glided past the town of N., where they were laid to rest, till "all that are in the graves shall hear the voice of the Son of God and shall come forth; they that have done good, to the resurrection of life; and they that have done evil, to the resurrection of damnation." Thus passed away a young man of brilliant talents, of great energy of character, devotedly attached to his profession, cut down when his hopes were high of attaining an eminence as a lawyer. Unfortunately he had received the wrong training in his childhood and youth, and when he grew up to manhood he read infidel books—embraced their sentiments, and discarded Christianity. Though he renounced infidelity in a dying hour, *he died in despair.*

CHAPTER XXIX.

JAMES EPPERSON.

In the Fall of 1840 the writer was appointed to Franklin circuit as preacher in charge. He was an entire stranger to the people to whom he was sent. The circuit was large, embracing all of Johnson, a large portion of Morgan, and parts of Marion, Bartholomew, and Brown counties.

Soon after the adjournment of Conference, the writer set out to explore his new circuit, and to procure a house in which he could place his family. The first night after entering the bounds of his circuit he spent at the house of a local elder, of some years' standing, who gave him a general account of the circuit, and plied him pretty closely with questions in theology and Church law, but could give him no information as to where he could obtain a house for his family, and did not seem to take much interest in that subject; he, however, warned the "new preacher" faithfully against " *one James Epperson*," who lived down toward the southern boundary of the circuit, telling me to have nothing to do with him, saying, "If he hears that you are in search of a house for your family, he will very likely offer you some accommodations, making great promises as to what he will do; but you need not rely upon any promise he makes, for he will not fulfill one of them."

The next morning the writer started on his way with a heavy heart. The account he had received of his circuit was by no means flattering, and the warning he had received in regard to "one James Epperson" weighed heavily on his mind. He took his course through the center of his circuit, traveling toward the southern portion. As he passed along he inquired of all the Methodists he found for a house wherein he could place his family, but no tidings of one could be obtained.

In the evening of the third day he arrived at Morgantown. Here he met his colleague, Rev. Jacob Myers. No house could be obtained in Morgantown. The next morning he and his colleague concluded to start regularly around the circuit, preaching where they could gather a congregation, leaving appointments for Mr. Myers, and perhaps they would hear of a house that could be obtained. On the third day thus spent, having collected a small congregation for preaching, during the delivery of the sermon, an elderly man, low of stature, rather corpulent, dressed in homespun jeans of walnut-brown color, with a bald head on a short neck, made his appearance and took a seat. As soon as the services were closed, the congregation being dismissed, the elderly man dressed in homespun, with a bald head, approached the writer, and inquired if he was the preacher in charge of the circuit. Being answered in the affirmative, he said, "I wish to speak to you a moment." They passed out of the house to a private place. The old man said, "I understand you are in search of a house for your family to live in this year. I have a house on my little farm, about ten miles distant from this, which you can have if you will accept it. The house in which I live is one of your preaching-places. If you will bring your family and occupy the vacant house on my place, you shall have it rent free, and your firewood shall cost you nothing."

He made sundry other promises as to what he would do if his offer was accepted. His name was asked for. He answered, "James Epperson." It flashed upon the writer's mind like lightning, "This is the very man of whom I was so faithfully warned by that local elder where I staid the first night I spent in the bounds of the circuit. He told me this man would make great promises as to what he would do, but he *would not* fulfill one of them." After a moment's pause, I told the old gentleman I would consider the matter, and let him know after dinner. I sought an interview with my colleague, Mr. Myers, and laid the whole case before him, telling him what the local elder had said in regard to Mr. Epperson. Mr. Myers advised me to go with the old man and see what the prospect was. After dinner we mounted our horses and set out for Mr. Epperson's residence. When we arrived darkness had closed in. On entering the cabin the writer found a family of seven or eight sons and daughters, from those pretty well grown up down to those of three or four years of age. The old lady was clad in homespun linsey-woolsey. The furniture was of the most primitive style, the whole family occupying the one room for cooking, eating, and sleeping.

Being weary in body and gloomy in mind I did not go to see what accommodations were afforded my faithful horse. Mrs. Epperson prepared a bountiful supper, which consisted of pork, bread, butter, milk, coffee, etc. The evening till "bedtime" was spent in hearing from Mr. Epperson an account of the circuit and the state of the Church, which was quite encouraging. In family prayer that night the writer felt that there was some *genuine religion* in that family, whatever else might be lacking. Mr. Epperson's cabin stood on the brow of a hill, the ground still gradually ascending for some distance above it.

After breakfast in the morning, the old gentleman proposed to go and "show the preacher" the house he had spoken of. Starting, they passed to the summit of the hill. There stood a comfortable stable, in which was the preacher's horse having plenty of hay and corn. As they drew near "Charlie" neighed to his master, as much as to say, "*I* have fared finely through the night; this is a good place for *me*." Seeing that Charlie was all right they passed into a field of ripe corn, the girdled forest trees standing thickly. About midway of the cornfield, they came to a low cabin, fifteen feet square, with one door, one window without glass or sash, a stick and clay chimney, which had partly fallen down, the cabin filled with corn fodder. Mr. Epperson said, "This is the house; rather a bad-looking chance, aint it?" I answered, "It is *not* very inviting in its appearance." "If you will come here and live I will repair the house and make it comfortable," responded Mr. Epperson; "but if you will come with me I will show you where *I* want it." They returned to the summit of the hill near where the stable containing the preacher's horse stood. The old man said, "This is where *I* want the house placed; if you will come here and live I will move it to this spot, and make it warm and comfortable, and [pointing to the stable] that shall be your stable; I built it to put preachers' horses in; no others have been in it, and never *shall* while I control it. You can bring your cow with you; your corn and hay through the year shall cost you nothing." The writer turned aside that he might spend a few moments in reflection. He soliloquized thus: "What shall I do? I have spent six days traveling through the circuit in search of a house for my family, and this is the only one offered me. This, too, is *the man* that local elder warned me to have nothing to do with, that he would not fulfill a promise that he made. What shall I do?" Something seemed to whisper in his ear, "This is the place; come here." I returned to the old man and told him I did not know what else to do than to accept his offer; there seemed to be no other opening for me to bring my family to the circuit, and Winter was rapidly setting in; that if I brought my family there, I would prefer to have the cabin where we stood, but it would require so much labor to remove it and place it there. Mr. Epperson said, "That is none of your business; if you say you will come here *I* will attend to all that." The writer said, "I will do it." Mr. Epperson inquired what day he could be ready to start with his family and goods. Pausing a moment, I said I thought I could be ready by a certain day. "Then," said the old man, "get upon your horse and go to your family as soon as you can; engage a team to bring part of your goods; get all things in readiness; I will be there with my wagon and team the night before." The writer bade the old man and his family good-by, mounted his horse and started for his family." At the time appointed Mr. Epperson was promptly on hand with his wagon and team. The next morning the goods and family were carefully stowed away in the two wagons. Bidding farewell to friends the preacher and his family started for their cabin home, at "one James Epperson's."

Late in the evening of the second day, in the midst of a snow-storm, they arrived at the place of their destination. Sure enough, there the cabin stood in its place, all right, and a large quantity of good seasoned firewood ranked up near by. It being too late to unload the wagons, the preacher and his family were most kindly entertained for the night at the cabin of Mr. Epperson. The next morning he assisted in placing all things "to rights" in the preacher's house. That being done he went to work and erected a shed over the door of the cabin, and placed a number of shelves near the door on the outside. When all was completed, he called the preacher's wife and said to her: "These shelves are for your cooking utensils, but this one is for your water-bucket. I want you to keep *it* sitting on that shelf day and night." It was soon discovered why he directed that the water-bucket should be kept upon that shelf day and night. The spring, where water was to be obtained, was some distance from the cabin, and to reach it you had to descend the hill upon which Mr. E.'s cabin stood and cross a branch, which made it laborious obtaining the necessary supply of water. Every morning when the preacher was absent upon his large circuit, and before the family were up, Mr. Epperson would have a bucket of water, fresh from the spring, sitting in its place upon the shelf.

After he had prepared the little accommodation of the shed and shelves, he erected a "lumber-room" at the end of the cabin, leaving an open passage between it and the cabin. When he had finished this room, he went to the preacher's wife and told her he wished her to keep the meat-tub, flour-barrel, and meal-chest in that "lumber-room." Through that open passage he always passed in going from his house into his fields to labor. Every few mornings, as he would be passing through to his work, he would turn into the lumber-room and look into the meat-tub, flour-barrel, and meal-chest. If he saw the contents of either getting low, you would soon see him with a sack, mounted on "Old Roan," starting for some distant neighborhood, not having said a word to the preacher's family as to what he was going to do. After some hours he would return with his sack well filled with meat, flour, or meal, as the necessity might require, often bringing other necessaries, such as maple sugar, molasses, dried fruit, etc. He delighted to accompany the preacher to his appointments on the circuit. On these occasions, wherever he went among the people, as there was but little money to be obtained for the preacher, he would ask them if they could not furnish him a ham of bacon, a sack of flour or meal. They often answered, "O yes; we would like to give brother S. a ham or two, or a sack of flour or meal"—whichever they could spare most conveniently—"but he lives so far away we don't know how to get it to him." Mr. Epperson's invariable reply was, "Never mind that; say he shall have it, and I will see that it is conveyed to him." Receiving a promise that whatever they proposed to furnish should be ready against a certain time, he would charge them to keep it till he called for it. Thus he knew where to go to obtain any of those articles for the preacher's family. In this way he kept them bountifully supplied throughout the year with the substantials of life. All the corn, hay, and firewood necessary for the preacher he furnished himself. The writer's family had not long been situated at this place till he, when away upon his large circuit, absent from them two and three weeks at a time, felt that under Mr. Epperson's care they would not be allowed to suffer.

Near the close of the Conference year, Mr. Epperson entered the preacher's cabin one evening, and said with some emotion, "I do not expect the Bishop will send you back to us another year, and, indeed, I could not ask him to do so. The circuit is a hard one to travel, and you have received but little pay." Addressing the writer's wife, he said, "You will want to go and see your father and mother while your husband has gone to Conference. Pack up all your things, and when he leaves for Conference I will take you and the children to your father's." And to the writer he said, "As soon as Conference adjourns write me, and let me know where you are sent—at what time and place to meet you with your goods, and I will bring them and your cow to you." The week before Conference was to commence the goods were carefully packed, and when I started to Conference Mr. Epperson started with my family to their friends, fifty miles distant.

At the close of Conference, a letter was addressed to Mr. Epperson, as he had requested, and accordingly on the evening of the day appointed, at the place specified, he was promptly on hand with the goods, the cow, and a fat hog, neatly dressed ready for use. The next morning, when he was about leaving, he was requested to receive some compensation for the much he had done for the preacher's family, but he refused, saying, "I have been an unprofitable servant. I have done nothing more than it was my duty to do." When he bade the preacher's wife farewell, he said to her, "Sister S., when you find another as good a friend to you as I have been, write to me." She never wrote. Though moving from place to place in the itinerancy, she has found many kind friends, she has often been heard to say, "I have never found *such* a friend as brother Epperson."

James Epperson was born and brought up in Kentucky. Up to manhood he had never attended a Methodist meeting, but had been taught rather to hate them. When he was a young man, he and several of his wicked associates concluded to attend a Methodist camp meeting which was to be held some miles distant, for frolic and fun. When the time arrived, they set out. On the way they made their arrangements and laid their plans for sport. They arrived at the encampment on Saturday, in the afternoon. As they drew near they heard the sound of singing, praying, groaning, crying, and rejoicing mingled in, to them, strange contrast. When they entered the inclosure of tents, a strange feeling came over young Epperson, and he began to tremble. Such a scene he had never beheld, and such sounds had never before fallen upon his ear. He approached near the altar, where a prayer meeting was going on, and took a seat. Ever and anon the shout of a new-born soul rose high above the songs, and groans, and prayers that were ascending from the altar. Young Epperson soon found his heart all broken up, and tears fast falling from his eyes—all thoughts of sport having left him. One of the preachers seeing him weeping and trembling approached and requested him to go into the altar, and let the pious pray for him. He consented, and, led by the preacher, he went in, and falling upon his knees commenced pleading for mercy. Before the sun arose the next morning the Sun of Righteousness had arisen upon him, dispelling all his moral darkness, pouring a flood of light, and joy, and peace into his soul. The holy Sabbath was a day of sacred peace such as he had never enjoyed before. He seemed to be in a new world. He *was* " a new man in Christ Jesus." He united with the Church and continued a faithful, devoted member to the day of his death.

After he had married a wife he came to Indiana and settled in Morgan county, where he spent the remainder of his days, serving his day and generation to the glory of God and the weal of the Church.

He was quite gifted in prayer, a tender class-leader, a kind neighbor, a generous, warm-hearted friend, devotedly attached to the Methodist Episcopal Church, ever ready to devote his time and means to her support. Several years since he quietly passed away to his home in heaven. The reader may, perhaps, desire to know *why* that local elder gave the writer such an account of "*one James Epperson.*" The reason is briefly this: that local elder and another local preacher in the circuit were "at outs," and Mr. Epperson was a friend of the other local preacher.

CHAPTER XXX.

HON. JAMES RARIDEN.

Mr. Rariden came to Indiana at an early day, and while he himself was yet a young man. He was about five feet seven or eight inches in hight, with a broad chest; high, well-developed forehead, black hair, thickly set upon his head; with keen black eyes. His left arm was withered and hung uselessly at his side. He usually carried it in a "sling." Though he had the use of but one arm, he performed manual labor till he arrived at manhood. It was said that he had split as many as two and three hundred rails in one day. He was a poor young man, having nothing to rely upon for support except his own energy and his own indomitable will. He had not enjoyed the advantages of a collegiate nor even an academical education, but by his own effort he succeeded in acquiring a very fair English education. When he came to Indiana he stopped in Wayne county, which was then new. Salisbury was the county seat. Here he made his first location. He soon obtained the place of deputy under David Hoover, who was then clerk of the county. This was his entrance into public life. Writing in the clerk's office, together with his attendance upon the courts, gave him a thirst for legal knowledge and a desire to be a lawyer. He wrote in the clerk's office for some two or three years. In this way he obtained quite an extensive knowledge of law and the manner of doing business in court, while at the same time his office as deputy clerk rendered him a competent support. During the time he was deputy clerk he devoted all his leisure hours to reading law, so that when he ceased to act in that capacity he was licensed to practice and admitted to the bar.

Mr. Rariden had a vigorous, active mind; could analyze a case presented to him, and knew well how to present the strong points in the cause of his client and the weak ones in the cause of the opposite party. He was surpassed by few, if any, in his skill in the examination of witnesses. In his cross-examinations, many a poor wight who undertook to swear *too* much, or to be *too* positive, found himself confused, confounded, overwhelmed, and in the midst of self-contradictions—his testimony destroyed. He had a pleasant voice and knew well how to use it. He spoke with great fluency and ease to himself, and was sometimes truly eloquent. Often when addressing a jury in a criminal case he would bring tears, like raindrops, from the eyes of the jurors. When he entered upon the practice of law he rose rapidly in his profession, and continued rising till he stood among the ablest in Indiana. He seldom lost a case. Such was his distinction as a lawyer that he was sought for with great eagerness by litigants. In a few years he accumulated by his profession a very handsome property.

When the county seat of Wayne was moved from Salisbury to Centerville, he removed his office to the latter place, and when he had well established himself in business, and accumulated a sufficient amount of property to justify him in taking to himself a wife, he married an amiable and intelligent young lady, the daughter of Judge John Test, of Lawrenceburg.

Mr. Rariden took an active part in the politics of the country. He was a very decided Whig of the Henry Clay school, and a great admirer of that distinguished statesman. He represented Wayne county several years in both houses of the State Legislature, and was twice elected to the lower house of the Congress of the United States. He was also a member of the State Convention which formed the present Constitution of Indiana. In each of these bodies he occupied a high position, and was considered an able debater. Unfortunately for Mr. Rariden and the country, he was not religious. Had he been, with his talents and influence, and the high position in the community which he occupied, he might have accomplished much good. He did not indulge in wickedness as many men of his profession did. His most common sin was profanity. To that he was much addicted. In a conversation with a friend, on one occasion, he very frankly confessed his great error in this particular, and related the following incident: One Sabbath day, in the Winter season, his wife and little son, who was some six years of age, went to Church, while he remained at home. After they had returned from Church, the family being seated around the fire, Mr. Rariden engaged in reading, his little son began to cry most bitterly. His mother asked him the cause. For some time there was hesitation. Being urged to tell what it was that so much grieved him, he said, "My pa will go to hell." His mother asked him what made him think so. He answered: "The preacher said to-day that all swearers will go to hell, and my pa swears." Mr. Rariden said it was the severest reproof he had ever received. It affected him much. He resolved then and there to make an effort to quit using profane language.

He was gentlemanly in all his intercourse with society, and always treated religious people and religious worship with great respect, and was quite a regular attendant upon the ministry of the Word. He was frequently heard to say, "I would not have my wife backslide or leave the Church for any consideration." His house was always open to ministers of the Gospel, and from himself and family they received a cordial welcome and a hospitable entertainment. He was liberal to the Church and all benevolent enterprises. He *abhorred* parsimoniousness. When the Rev. John Everhart traveled the old Whitewater circuit, he had the misfortune to lose his horse. Being a poor man, as Methodist preachers generally were in those days, and not able to purchase another, he was greatly embarrassed. Toward the close of the Conference year, a camp meeting was held at Doddridge's camp-ground, a few miles from Centerville. The circuit had fallen far behind in meeting the claims of the preachers. Mr. Everhart was without a horse, and there was not money enough brought in to pay for one, though horses were cheap. What was to be done? The official members concluded to get up a subscription-paper, and make an effort to raise a sufficient amount of money to procure a horse for Mr. Everhart. Accordingly, a subscription-paper was drawn in due form, and several names were put down, with the amount varying from twenty-five to fifty cents. They then started round the camp-ground to see what they could do. They soon came to Mr. Rariden, who was then a young lawyer rapidly rising in his profession. To him they presented the paper and politely requested him to subscribe. He took the paper and read it, with the names and amount attached. After a moment's pause, he said, "No, not one cent will I subscribe on this paper. Do you expect to raise money enough to pay for a horse for Mr. Everhart with such subscriptions as these?" Turning to a gentleman who stood near, he said, "Mr. A., what will you take for that fine horse you bought the other day?" "What do you want with him?" asked the gentleman. "It is none of your business," said Mr. Rariden. "What will you take for him? is the question." "I bought him for my own use," said Mr. A. "I gave seventy-five dollars for him. If you want him for Mr. Everhart you shall have him for sixty-five." "Hand him over to Mr. Everhart," said Mr. Rariden, "and I will pay you the money when I return to Centerville;" then tearing up the subscription-paper he threw it upon the ground, saying, "Go to —— with your subscription-paper." The horse was handed over to the preacher, and Mr. Rariden paid for him. This act of liberality raised him in the estimation of the public, and, doubtless, brought him professional business; but it is not to be supposed that he did it for that purpose. He had a liberal soul, and seeing the small amounts subscribed by others, and believing the object a good one, he made the preacher a present of the horse. In this he gave an exhibition of one trait in his character.

So far as is known to the writer, he never connected himself with any branch of the Christian Church. His preferences were for the Methodist Episcopal Church. His residence was in Wayne county from the time he came to Indiana to the close of his life. He was a favorite with her citizens. He lived to a somewhat advanced age, and died a few years since, much respected.

CHAPTER XXXI.

AN ECCENTRIC CIRCUIT STEWARD.

A. M. C. G. resided in the town of B. He was a member of the Methodist Episcopal Church, and one of the stewards of the circuit. A. K., who was also a circuit steward, lived in the same town. The circuit in which the town of B. was situated had been districted so that each steward had his portion to attend to, financially. The town of B. was in the district assigned to Mr. K. as steward. The people were not very liberal in paying their "quarterage," and Mr. K. could not bring them to the proper standard. Mr. G. having acquired quite a reputation for making "quarterage speeches," Mr. K. requested him, at different times, to make a quarterage speech to his people, but Mr. G. persistently declined. The appointment for circuit preaching in B. was on a week-day.

On one occasion when the preacher in charge of the circuit had arrived in B.—it was on the morning of the day he was to preach in the place—the class-leader came to him with a list of the names of some fifteen or twenty members who were delinquent in attendance on class meeting, and desired him to attend to them "under the rule," that day after preaching. Heading the delinquent list stood the name of Mr. G., the steward. The class-leader informed the preacher that the other delinquents hid behind Mr. G.; that they refused to attend class meeting till the steward did, and that he could not get him to go to class meeting. When the class-leader had made an end of the presentation of delinquents, the preacher stepped across the street to the shop of Mr. G. and informed him of the complaint entered by the leader, and showed him the list. He told him what the leader had said in regard to the other delinquent members hiding behind him, refusing to attend class meeting till he did. The preacher labored to impress the steward with a sense of the evil influence of his example, telling him that it would be a painful thing to have to exclude him from the Church "for willful neglect of class meeting," but that such *would be* the result if he did not reform. He also told him that he would that day, after preaching, retain the members of the Church, and call over the names of those who were delinquent and see if they would promise reformation. While the preacher was lecturing Mr. G., he stood and listened attentively, but did not utter a word. As soon as the preacher was through, he threw off his apron and went across the street to Mr. K.'s store, and said to him, "Brother K., I'll make that quarterage speech for you to-day, if you wish me to." Said Mr. K., "I wish you would, brother G.; indeed, I will be very much obliged to you if you will." And so the two brethren made their arrangements accordingly.

When the hour for preaching arrived, and the people began to collect at the small log church, Mr. G. came in with his Bible under his arm, and took a seat. At the close of the sermon the preacher requested the members of the Church to remain for a short space after the benediction was pronounced. While those who were not members of the Church were retiring, Mr. G. went to the preacher and said, "Brother S., I am going to make a quarterage speech for brother K. to-day; I want you to let me make *my speech* before you attend to your business." He insisted so earnestly that he might be allowed to do so, that the preacher consented. When all had become quiet, Mr. G. arose, and, addressing those present, informed them what he proposed doing. He opened his Bible, read several texts of Scripture, and proceeded to explain them, as teaching the duty of the people to support the Gospel. When he had explained and enforced all his texts, he added, "Our class-leader has presented to the preacher a list of the names of fifteen or twenty persons who do not attend class meeting, and he is going to attend to their cases to-day. *My* name stands at the head of that list. Brother S. came to see me this morning. He told me that the leader represented that those delinquent persons were hiding behind me; that is, refusing to attend class meeting because I do not, saying, 'Make your steward go to class, then

AN ECCENTRIC CIRCUIT STEWARD.

we will go.' Brother S. said if I did not attend class meeting the Church would be under the necessity of 'laying me aside.' He gave me a pretty good scourging, but did not give me a lick amiss. I did not say any thing to him. I reserved it all for you. You all know I once was class collector for this class; that I did come regularly to class meeting; that I never professed to be *very* religious. When at class you got happy and shouted, till I expected to see the shingles fly off the old meeting-house. You know I never shouted any. When class meeting closed and I asked you for your quarterage you were almost angry enough to destroy me. Thus it continued till I came to the conclusion that I was doing *you* a harm, and I knew that you were doing *me* a harm; that you had one kind of religion and I had another. Your religion made you *shout*, but did not make you pay your preacher, while my religion made me *pay my preacher*, but did not make me shout, and so I concluded to quit attending class, thinking my religion was better than yours. Now, the preacher says I will have to be expelled from the Church if I do not attend class, and I tell *you* I am not going to be expelled from the Church. Henceforth I am coming to class, and by the grace of God every time you *shout* I'll *dun* you for quarterage." From the time Mr. G. made that speech the class at B. sent up to the quarterly conference an enlarged financial report.

CHAPTER XXXII.

REV. L. W. BERRY, D. D.

Lucien William Berry was born in Alburgh, or Alburg, Vermont, in 1815. His parents were members of the Baptist Church. His father was a physician of some eminence; he bestowed much attention on the cultivation of the mind of his son. At a very early age Lucien exhibited aptness to learn, and a fondness for books. He had a retentive memory, and retained well what he read.

While he was a boy his father moved to Ohio. Here, in the fourteenth year of his age, he was converted and united with the Methodist Episcopal Church. After his conversion, his thirst for knowledge increased. He divided his time between the study of the sciences and the reading of religious books. Such were his piety and talents that in the seventeenth year of his age he was licensed to preach. Rev. W. B. Christie, who was presiding elder of the district where young Berry lived at the time he was licensed to preach, saw his brilliant talents and promising usefulness, and took him under his special care, pointing out a course of theological study for him. The kindness of Mr. Christie to young Berry was such as to cause him ever afterward to look upon him as his best earthly friend. There was no living man he so much admired.

In the Fall of 1833, Mr. Christie, who was then presiding elder of Wooster district, in Ohio, employed young Berry, who was then but eighteen years of age, to travel Roscoe circuit with Rev. J. M'Dowel, who was preacher in charge. Mr. M'Dowel took the young preacher into his kind embrace, and instructed him in all the duties of an itinerant Methodist preacher. Their hearts became closely united in the strongest bonds of Christian and ministerial affection, which time did not weaken nor changing circumstances sever. Here young Berry commenced his itinerancy, and labored through the year with great acceptability to the people. His youth, zeal, and talents attracted much attention, and often brought crowds to hear him preach. Though the circuit was large, requiring much traveling on horseback, he pursued his studies closely. He read *Watson's Institutes* so attentively that by the close of the year he could repeat a large portion of both volumes *memoriter*.

About the close of this year, an incident occurred which made an impression upon his mind that never left him. He attended a camp meeting which was held in another part of the district from that where he had been laboring. His youthful ears had not been altogether deaf to the praises bestowed upon him as a preacher. He felt some anxiety to maintain the reputation he had acquired at the camp meeting to which he was going. Accordingly, he prepared a sermon, which led him to draw largely from Watson's Institutes. He studied his sermon till he thought he had it "at his tongue's end." Thus armed and equipped he went to the camp meeting, feeling very confident of success when his time should come to stand before the congregation. On Saturday, in the afternoon, the presiding elder appointed him to preach. The congregation which assembled at the stand to hear the young preacher was large. He gave out his hymn intrepidly—the congregation joined in singing. At the close of the hymn he kneeled in prayer. Rising from his knees he announced his text. He had uttered but a few sentences when he began to falter and "catch at his words." Darkness overspread his mind. He forgot, for the time being, all he had thought upon the subject. After a few minutes' vainly struggling to recover his thoughts, he was compelled to give it up and take his seat overwhelmed with confusion. His kind presiding elder arose, and, as he was capable of doing, took up the subject and delivered a powerful discourse. Young Berry was so mortified he could not remain in the stand. He retired to the preachers' tent, took his hat, made his way to a secluded place in the woods, where he remained alone till after nightfall.

The next morning the presiding elder appointed him to preach the first sermon for the day. He begged to be excused, saying he "could not preach." The presiding elder said, "If *you* can't, the Lord can *through* you, and you must try. You were anxious to preach on yesterday. You went in your own strength and failed; now go in the strength of the Lord and he will help you." Finding there was no excuse to be accepted by the elder, he took his Bible and once more sought seclusion in the woods, where, in great agony of mind, he poured out his soul in prayer till the hour for preaching arrived. At the signal to call the people together for worship, he returned to the encampment. With much trembling and fear he went upon the stand and commenced the opening services. In his prayer he threw himself wholly upon the Lord. With a tremulous voice he read his text. He had not proceeded far till all fear of man left him, and with his eye fixed upon the glory of God in the salvation of souls, he passed through to the close of his sermon. The congregation was greatly moved, and tears fell fast from many eyes.

At the close of this Conference year, 1834, he was admitted on trial in the Ohio Conference, and appointed junior preacher to Oxford circuit. At the close of the year he discontinued, and entered Miami University as a student. In this institution he made rapid advancement. During his residence at Oxford he was united in marriage to Miss Adaline Fay. He did not remain in the University to complete his collegiate course, but he laid the foundation of an education which he afterward pursued without the aid of an instructor till he took high rank among learned men. After spending a few sessions at the University, he determined to again enter the itinerancy. In the Fall of 1838 he was admitted on trial in the Indiana Conference and appointed in charge of Noblesville circuit. Here the writer saw him for the first time, and formed his acquaintance, which ripened into friendship and intimacy—an intimacy closer than he ever enjoyed with any other man.

Mr. Berry spent two years on this circuit, and was much admired and esteemed by the people. At this time Campbellism was rife in that region. By request, Mr. Berry preached a sermon on baptism, in Noblesville, which was such a staggering blow to exclusive immersion that the friends of that theory rallied to its support to save it from its fall. In a short time after the delivery of that sermon, Mr. Berry received a challenge from Rev. F. W. Emmons, a disciple of Alexander Campbell, for a public debate on the mode of baptism. Mr. Berry respectfully declined to accept the challenge in a private letter to Mr. Emmons, in which he assigned his reasons for so doing. That private letter Emmons published, in a garbled form, with his comments, making many misrepresentations. In reply to these misrepresentations, Mr. Berry published a pamphlet of forty pages, entitled, "The Deformer Reformed; or Corruption Exposed: being an address to the people of Noblesville, to which is prefixed a correct copy of the letter published by F. W. Emmons." In this pamphlet Mr. Berry displayed much forensic skill, and showed himself to be a controversialist of no ordinary grade. The influence of this publication was to silence, to a great extent, the assaults hitherto made upon the Methodist Episcopal Church in that place. During the two years Mr. Berry labored on Noblesville circuit he greatly endeared himself to the people, and when he left them they felt that they were losing the services of a minister of superior mind, talents, and maturity for one of his age.

In the Fall of 1840 he was appointed to Knightstown circuit. Here he labored with much success. The people in crowds waited on his ministry.

In Knightstown Universalism had made a lodgment, and many of the people were being carried away by it. Mr. Berry considered it to be his duty to take off the specious garb with which that system had clothed itself, and exhibit it in its true character. This he proceeded to do in a few sermons of great clearness and power. These discourses produced great excitement among the Universalists. The result was, a preacher of that persuasion, by the name of M'Cuen, challenged Mr. Berry to a public discussion of the question, "Will all men be holy and happy in a future state?" M'Cuen to affirm, and Berry to deny. The challenge was accepted, the time for the debate to come off fixed upon, and the rules by which they were to be governed in the discussion arranged. The excitement now ran high. The Universalists were *sure* of a great victory. Their champion, M'Cuen, was an old theological pugilist, having held thirty-four debates with ministers of different denominations, while Berry was a young man and had never held a public debate, but had spent the most of his time since eighteen years of age in traveling large circuits as a Methodist itinerant preacher, and had not had the advantage of even attending a public debate. The contest appeared an unequal one, and some of Mr. Berry's friends feared to have him meet that *ecclesiastical gladiator*. When the time for the commencement of the debate arrived, the crowd in attendance was so great that no church in town would hold them. The discussion was held in a grove. Several Universalist preachers were present to assist their champion as armor-bearers. The debate continued three days. By the close of the first day all fear upon the part of Mr. Berry's friends was dissipated, and they were proud that they had such a youthful defender of the truth. His closing speech, in which he summed up the arguments that had been advanced, was most overwhelming, bearing every thing before it. His soul seemed to catch inspiration from on high; his lips and tongue were touched anew with a live coal from off God's altar, and his words burned as they fell upon the audience. M'Cuen and his friends turned pale. At the close of the debate, Mr. Berry and his friends proposed to publish the speeches made in the discussion, a stenographer having been employed to take them down, but Mr. M'Cuen and his friends would not consent.

The next year Mr. Berry was appointed to Rushville circuit. Here he labored faithfully to the close of the year, making many warm friends, losing none of his reputation, as a zealous, faithful minister, of superior talents.

In the Fall of 1842 he was stationed at Wesley Chapel, Indianapolis, where he remained two years. At this time Rev. Henry Ward Beecher, now of Brooklyn, N. Y., who was rapidly rising to his zenith as a pulpit orator, was pastor of the Second Presbyterian Church. His church and Mr. Berry's stood within a stone's cast of each other. Though the latter had to stand up in the pulpit by the side of this young Demosthenes, he gathered a large congregation of admiring hearers, who waited upon his ministry from Sabbath to Sabbath.

At the close of his second year in the capital he was appointed presiding elder of Indianapolis district, which he traveled two years, and was then appointed presiding elder of Brookville district, which he traveled three years.

In the Summer of 1849 the Joint Board of Trustees and Visitors of Indiana Asbury University elected him President of that institution, to succeed Dr. Simpson. He continued to travel his district till the close of the Conference year, and then assumed the responsibilities of the Presidency. While he held this high position the degree of Doctor of Divinity was conferred upon him by the Ohio Wesleyan University. In discharging the duties of President of Asbury, he brought all the powers of his great mind into requisition, devoting all his energies day and night to the interests of the institution, and to the advancement of the young men committed to his care. He drew them to him by the strongest chords of esteem and affection. As an evidence of this, we give the following extract from a letter written since his death, by one who had been a student under him, which now lies before us:

"While the whole connection will join me in lamentation that one so able to defend has fallen from the walls of Zion, and has resigned his silver trumpet to another, we know not whom, none but those who have enjoyed the advantages of his counsel and faithful instructions during college life, felt the power of his genius and the fervor of his zeal, will fully appreciate my bereavement. His mind, his countenance, and all his bearing, stand before me an image of inimitable greatness. We shall no more hear his fervid eloquence, that came as the dashing of Niagara's waves, nor feel the joy that his image imparted when it spoke its approval of a virtuous act."

Dr. Berry was President of Indiana Asbury University five years, when he resigned his position in that institution and was stationed in Centenary Church, New Albany. Though eleven years had elapsed since he had been engaged directly in the pastoral work, he had lost none of his zeal, nor had he forgotten how to do that particular species of Christian labor, such as conducting prayer meetings, meeting the classes, visiting families, etc.

During this year he was elected President of Iowa Wesleyan University, and in July, 1855, entered upon his duties as the head of that institution. Here he labored four years with success, the institution constantly rising under his superintendency, the faculty and students feeling that a master-mind was among them.

The leading Methodists of the State of Missouri, together with the citizens of Jefferson City, determined on founding a university of the first class at that city, and several large donations were made as a basis upon which to start the enterprise.

In looking over the whole Church for the man best qualified to take charge of this grand enterprise and carry it through to completion, Dr. Berry was selected, and was, by the Board of Trustees, elected President and Financial Agent. After mature consideration and a great mental struggle, by the advice of some of the most prominent men of the Church, he concluded, for the sake of the Methodist Episcopal Church and the cause of education, to accept the position. The faculty and students of the Iowa Wesleyan University were loth to give him up. From a letter which now lies before me, written by one of their number since the death of Dr. Berry, we quote the following: "It was with great reluctance, with fear and trembling, that we gave him up to enter upon his last field of labor, from which death so recently called him. He went, but not without our sympathies and prayers. But little did we think his warfare was so nearly ended; his victory so surely won." In 1857 he took his position at the head of the Missouri enterprise, and entered upon the arduous duties devolved upon him. He was not permitted to prosecute the work to completion. An inscrutable Providence ordered otherwise. He had prosecuted this work but a brief space when he was prostrated by affliction. In November, 1857, he was attacked with asthma and erysipelas combined, which produced paralysis of the tongue, throat, cheeks, and lips, depriving him almost wholly of speech and the power to swallow medicine or nourishment. In this condition, enduring great suffering, he lingered about nine months, and died at the house of John G. Ruckle, Esq., in the city of Cincinnati, whither he had gone to obtain medical assistance, on the morning of the twenty-third of July, 1858. Being deprived so nearly of the power of speech, he could not converse much, but he wrote many letters to his distant friends. This he continued to do almost daily up to the period of his death. In these letters he expresses his unshaken confidence in God, though passing through the furnace of affliction. In a letter written to a friend a few days before his death, he says, "My soul has been staid upon the Lord, and from day to day I rejoice in his goodness. This letter costs me much pain. I write with difficulty, and it is all about myself—a very unworthy object. But Jesus is worthy."

When the taper of life burned out, his soul quietly passed away to join the redeemed at God's right hand. His remains were conveyed to Indianapolis, where a funeral discourse was delivered to a large and weeping audience by Rev. James Havens, after which they were interred in the old cemetery near the city. Dr. Berry was one of the closest students—going to the bottom of every subject he undertook to investigate. He was an intellectual giant. He never allowed himself to go into the pulpit without having thoroughly studied the subject he expected to present to the people. He wrote sketches of all his sermons, but seldom took one into the pulpit. At his quarterly meetings, when he was presiding elder, after having gone through with the labors of Saturday and Saturday night, when all others had retired to rest, he would take the manuscript containing a sketch of the sermon he designed preaching the next day, place it upon the mantle before him, then walk the room and study, with much prayer, for hours. The next day, when he appeared before the congregation, his sermon seldom failed to tell upon the people.

Rev. Allen Wiley once remarked, "Such mental efforts as Berry makes in preaching are enough to prostrate the physical system of any man." It is possible that his wonderful mental efforts did induce his early death. If so, he fell a sacrifice to his Master's cause.

He was a wise administrator of Discipline, whether in charge of circuits, stations, or districts. He was no time severe, but fearlessly announced his sentiments where and whenever it was necessary for him to do so. To a stranger, there seemed to be something in his appearance which said, "Don't come too close;" but he had a kind heart, warm friendship, and strong attachments to his friends.

As a preacher he had few equals, and no superior in this country. All his sermons evinced much thought, and were often overwhelming in their effects. Sometimes the people sat awe-stricken as if incapable of moving. At other times, they were so thrilled with joy that the loud alleluias would roll up simultaneously from many voices, drowning the voice of the speaker. At a camp meeting held near Cumberland, in Marion county, in the Fall of 1842, he preached on Sunday morning to an audience of several thousand, from, "Acquaint now thyself with him and be at peace; thereby good shall come unto thee." As he advanced in his sermon, the tide of feeling in the vast audience rose higher and higher, till he reached his last proposition. While describing the *good* that should result from an acquaintance with God, some one gave expression to the thrill of joy that filled the soul. Instantly, hundreds arose to their feet, clapped their hands, and shouted aloud the praises of the Redeemer, so completely drowning the voice of the preacher that he took his seat. There was no more preaching at the camp meeting that day. The remaining hours and a large portion of the night were spent in singing, praying, and praising the Lord. Thirty-eight united with the Church as the result of that day's labor.

As an educator Dr. Berry had few superiors. Such were his pulpit talents, and such his ability as an administrator of Discipline, that many of his friends thought it was a mistake in him to leave the regular work and confine himself to the labors of a literary institution. The opportunities for doing good in such an institution are numerous and great, but the itinerancy is the great field for usefulness.

He enjoyed the confidence of his brethren in the ministry to a high degree. He was three times elected delegate to the General Conference, twice from the Indiana, and once from the Iowa Conference. He was looked to by many ministers and private members as a promising man for the Episcopacy, and would doubtless, had he lived a few years longer, been called to that high position in the Church.

He was highly esteemed by his numerous friends, and their sorrow was deep when his voice was hushed in death. The following is taken from a letter published in one of our Church papers, giving an account of the closing scene in the first session of the Iowa Conference held after the death of Dr. Berry:

"The occasion was unusually solemn, and mournfully melancholy. One of the brightest stars in the constellation of Christianity; one of the purest lights in the firmament of Methodism has reached to another orbit. The sun of our dearly-beloved brother, Rev. L. W. Berry, D. D., went gently down to rise with greater beauty and upon a clearer sky in a better world. His death was known to us all. Our stricken hearts were yet bleeding from the wounds inflicted by the hand of the ruthless, unyielding monster. Mt. Pleasant, his former home, was draped in mourning, and the bereaved Church and his own orphan children were called as mourners to the altar of his own place of worship to lament his departure.

"The announcement of his death was formally made by Rev. Joseph Brooks, A. M., of the Central Christian Advocate, who briefly addressed the Conference in nearly the following words: 'I have to announce the death of my dearest earthly friend, one bound to me by every tie of Christian love and fraternal affection. He died a martyr to a great cause. He had the frame and muscular power of a giant, yet he spared them not in the work of the Lord. His clarion voice was like a trumpet in the proclamation of the unsearchable riches of the Gospel of the grace of our Lord Jesus Christ. With his mind well stored he had not a treasure or a jewel which was not fully emptied into the treasury of the Lord; but above all was his great heart given to the work of the Lord. He lived in the midst of wealth, yet he chose to die poor, unincumbered with the cares of the world. He could have joined any profession, would have been an ornament to any society, and was well-qualified for any position in Church or State. But he chose rather to suffer affliction with the people of God. In the mysteries of holiness he had been a lifetime-student, but in the closing days of his life he was a model of Christian experience, of Christian purity. His like I shall scarcely look upon again. He was my friend and I loved him. He has passed away and I shall meet him in heaven.'

"Brother Brooks was followed by Rev. C. Elliott, D. D. The Doctor spoke warmly of their first acquaintance, of the powers of mind, the kindness of heart, and great usefulness of Dr. Berry during life, and of his triumph in death. It was affecting to see this venerable servant of God moved to tears, and with the simplicity of a child referring thus to his departed friend.

"Rev. J. W. M'Dowel next spoke of taking Dr. Berry when a boy of seventeen into the ministry, how he labored, how he lived. Brother M'Dowel was so moved he sat down bathed in tears.

"Brother Hardy called back the recollections of his own conversion through the ministry of Dr. Berry.

"Brother Bradley spoke of the kind encouragement given him in the youth of his ministry by Dr. Berry.

"Bishop Morris arose and with great solemnity remarked, 'In the year 1842, when I was holding the Indiana Conference, which then embraced the whole of the State of Indiana, I asked the presiding elders, before any appointment was made, to tell me, leaving all personal considerations out of the question, who was the best and most active available station preacher in the Indiana Conference. They responded without a dissenting voice, Lucien W. Berry. I then put him down for the charge in Indianapolis, the most difficult charge in the Conference. A great man and a prince has fallen. Dr. Berry was a great man. Of course I would not say this if he were present. He was of the first class of pulpit men in America. He has gone, and I trust we shall all meet him up yonder,' (pointing to the heavens.)

"And thus closed these solemn services."

Dr. Berry did not profess to be perfect, nor do his friends claim perfection for him, but all who knew him considered him a "burning and a shining light," a man of deep piety, one who had laid his all on God's altar, a star of the first magnitude. Most of his ministerial life was spent in Indiana, and Indiana is honored with his grave. It was a mysterious providence that one of so much promise should be cut down in the prime of life, that so brilliant a luminary should set just as it was reaching its meridian. "But God's ways are not our ways."

In this brief sketch of Dr. Berry we have not pretended to write his biography, only to pay a small tribute of respect to the memory of a dear, intimate, and long-tried friend. We have more than one hundred letters written by him in a private correspondence of nearly twenty years' continuance. We might have selected many passages from these letters which would have been interesting, showing the state of his mind at different times, his views upon different subjects, and the warm friendship of his heart; but to have done so would have extended this sketch beyond the proper limits of such a notice. Dr. Berry will never be forgotten by those who knew him well.

CHAPTER XXXIII.

REV. JAMES HAVENS.

In attempting to write a sketch of Rev. James Havens, we feel our inadequacy to present such a portrait of him as his long life, abundant labors, extensive usefulness, and great worth demand; and yet, we can not consent to leave him unnoticed. A long and intimate acquaintance seem to demand that we should pay some humble tribute of respect to his memory. We knew him when we were in our juvenile years; our father's house was his home; he and our father were fast friends, united in heart like David and Jonathan, and they are, doubtless, now together before the throne. We delighted to do him reverence; to take care of his horse, and in every possible way to administer to his comfort. He was for four years consecutively our presiding elder. We have followed him as he led the way on many a moral battle-field, and have witnessed many a glorious victory achieved by him, through Jesus Christ, as the leader of God's sacramental hosts. We are sorry we have so little data to write from. The lamented Dr. L. W. Berry, some years since, commenced writing the biography of father Havens. Many interesting incidents in his early life Dr.

Berry had noted down, as he received them from his lips. Other pressing duties prevented him from completing the work, and since his death the manuscript can not be found. This is much to be regretted. There were some things in the life of father Havens, contained in that manuscript, that had never been given to the world, which are now, perhaps, forever lost, biographer and subject both having passed away from the busy scenes of this life. We have heard Dr. Berry read portions of his manuscript, but can not undertake to reproduce from memory.

James Havens was born in Mason county, Kentucky, December 25, 1791. He was the son of John and Nancy Havens. His parents were not educated persons, but possessed vigorous minds. His father had a strong, elastic, physical constitution, and lived to an advanced age. His mother died when he was young, and his father married again. He cherished the fondest recollections of his mother, though she was taken from him when he was a small boy.

In 1805 his father emigrated to Ohio, he being in the fourteenth year of his age. All his early life was spent in a new country, in the backwoods. This subjected him to many disadvantages, but there were some advantages; these were turned to good account. He was deprived of the advantages of schools and the means of mental culture, but his having been brought up under the toils and hardships of a life upon the frontier, developed his physical powers, made him bold and fearless in what he undertook to do, and taught him self-reliance. This assisted to prepare him for the work that was before him.

In 1811 he was united in marriage to Miss Anna Higgenbotham. Their union proved to be a most happy one. They lived together in uninterrupted connubial bliss for many years, she acting well her part in all the vicissitudes of life. They reared up a large family of children in respectability. Three of their sons, Landy, George, and David, became itinerant Methodist preachers.

In 1811, soon after he was married, he was converted and united with the Methodist Episcopal Church under the ministry of Rev. James B. Finley. It has been stated that he was the first person Mr. Finley received into the Church after he entered the itinerancy. From the time of his conversion and union with the Church, he turned his attention entirely to the subject of religion and the salvation of souls, except what was absolutely necessary to meet the wants of his family. It was not long till he felt that a dispensation of the Gospel was committed unto him—that "Woe is me if I preach not the Gospel!" His want of an education and an abiding sense of his own weakness—of his lack of qualification for the work of the ministry—a calling so high and holy, made him tremble and caused him great distress of mind. He was often made to exclaim, "Lord, I can not preach! I am willing to do any thing I can do. How can I preach?" But wherever he went, by day and by night, "Woe is me if I preach not the Gospel!" was sounding in his ears. He has often been heard to say in the latter years of his life, that he did not believe any man ought to be allowed to preach who did not feel that everlasting woe would be his portion if he did not—that it was trifling with sacred things—a crime for any man to enter the work of the ministry merely as a profession. The idea of any man's choosing it for himself was in his estimation most erroneous. He believed God chose that work for certain men, and called them to it by impressing the fact so deeply upon their minds as to make them feel, "*Woe* is me if I preach not the Gospel!" After some months of groaning and sighing, he yielded, and was in the same year in which he was married and united with the Church, licensed to preach. He was a local preacher ten years, preaching as often as he could, having to labor for the support of his family.

In 1821 he was admitted on trial in the Ohio Conference, and appointed to Salt Creek circuit. In 1822 he was appointed to Straight Creek circuit. In 1823 he was received into full connection and ordained elder, having been ordained deacon as a local preacher. This year he was appointed to Brush Creek circuit, with Rev. Henry B. Bascom preacher in charge. This was to him an important year in his ministerial and itinerant life. Here he formed an intimate acquaintance with and a friendship for Mr. Bascom that was never broken off. By an intimate and close association with him he discovered that he had been misjudged by many persons who thought him to be proud and aristocratic in his feelings. He found him to be a most humble and deeply-pious minister. His association with Mr. Bascom this year was of great advantage to him in his ministry.

In 1824 he was transferred to the Illinois Conference, and appointed to Connersville circuit. This was his introduction into the State of Indiana. He located his family on some wild land he had purchased in Rush county, not far from Rushville. In this vicinity his family ever afterward resided, while he traveled circuits and districts near and remote. Some were wont to censure him for keeping his family *local*, while he was a *traveling* preacher. Had he moved his family from year to year, he would have broken down and been compelled to locate. His family was large. He and his good wife were blessed with fifteen children. To have dragged these from circuit to circuit every year would have consumed a handsome fortune, when his quarterage receipts ranged from thirty to one hundred dollars per year. By locating his family on his own land where they could find employment, and where he could occupy what little time he had to spend with them in improving and cultivating his farm, and by the industry, frugality, and economy of his excellent wife he continued in the itinerancy, gave his children a fair education, supported them decently, and accumulated a handsome little property upon which he and his wife could lean for support in the time of old age. When and where did James Havens neglect his appropriate work because his family were located? The abundant blessings God bestowed upon him are evidences that his course was approbated by the Great Head of the Church.

In 1826 he was appointed to Whitewater circuit, where he traveled two years. In 1828 he was appointed to Rushville circuit. His health having to some extent failed, in consequence of his abundant labors, he was returned the next year to Rushville in charge as supernumerary, with a colleague to assist. In 1830, not having recovered his health, he was continued in a supernumerary relation and appointed in charge of Whitewater circuit with a colleague.

At the close of this year he was so broken down in health that notwithstanding his burning zeal in his Master's cause he was compelled to yield and take a superannuated relation. After resting a month or two, and recruiting his health a little, such was his unquenchable desire to be actively engaged to do something for the good of mankind and the glory of God that he took an agency from the "American Sunday School Union." In this department he labored till toward the close of the

Conference year, traveling quite extensively, organizing Sunday schools, and arousing the people on the subject of the great Sunday school enterprise. The next year, 1832, his relation was changed to that of supernumerary, and he was appointed Conference agent. In 1833 he was made effective, and appointed presiding elder of Madison district. The next year he was appointed presiding elder of Indianapolis district, where he continued four years. Having served the disciplinary term on the Indianapolis district, he was, in 1837, appointed agent for the "Preachers' Aid Society." At the close of this Conference year he was appointed presiding elder of Centerville district, and the next year to Connersville district. At the close of this year he was appointed to Indianapolis district, where he continued as presiding elder four years, when he was appointed to Rushville station. This had been his home since he came to Indiana. Here he had been preaching more or less each year for twenty years, and yet the people received him gladly. The next year he was stationed at Greensburg; in 1846 at Laurel. During this year his station was blessed with one of the most powerful revivals ever known in the Whitewater country. As the work continued from day to day it increased in interest and in power, till at the hour of service sinners by scores went forward to the altar without an invitation and kneeled down to be prayed for before the services had regularly commenced. Mr. Havens was returned to Laurel the following year. At the close of this year he was appointed to Greensburg district, which he traveled three years, and was then appointed presiding elder of Indianapolis district, which he traveled four years, when he was appointed Conference missionary.

Time and toil wore down his physical system till he was constrained to retire from the active work and take a superannuated relation, which he sustained to the close of his long and useful itinerant life. Though superannuated he did not cease preaching. He was called for in various places to assist at quarterly and protracted meetings, to preach funeral, missionary, and dedication sermons.

No man has done more for the moral and religious advancement of the citizens of Indiana than Mr. Havens. When he came to the State there was much wickedness—intemperance, gambling, and profanity. Against these and all other vices he took a decided stand, attacking them wherever he went. He shunned not to declare the whole counsel of God, "giving to saint and sinner their portion in due season." He was bold and resolute—was never known to quail before an enemy. If he did not succeed in accomplishing whatever he undertook, it was because he could not. He only failed after having put forth all his strength.

An incident occurred when he was a boy twelve or fourteen years of age which made a deep impression upon his mind and taught him a lesson that profited him in all after life—never to despair or cease his efforts to accomplish a good thing as long as he had any strength left. The family were moving. The country was new. They came to a river some two hundred yards wide which had to be ferried. The wagon and team, stock, and family had all been ferried across save James, who, for some reason, had been left behind. The ferry-boat had by some means become disabled, so that it could not be taken back after him. Night was approaching. There was no house near to which he could go for protection and shelter. There seemed to be no alternative but for James to swim the river or remain alone among ravenous beasts through the night, and till the boat could be repaired the next day. His father, speaking to him across the river, asked him "if he could swim it." He said he "would try." He put into the water. The current, which was rapid, carried him down stream. He became discouraged, finding his strength giving way. But his father walked slowly down the river on the bank for which he was struggling, and constantly encouraged him by saying, "Don't be discouraged, my son; you'll come out. Don't be discouraged, James; you'll reach the shore." These words of encouragement from his father nerved him afresh, and putting forth all his remaining strength he reached the shore much exhausted, and was assisted from the water by his father. This incident he frequently referred to in conversation in after life as being an important period in his life.

When he traveled a circuit in Ohio, there was one neighborhood in which the men generally were so rough and wicked that no one had made an effort to establish religious worship among them. Mr. Havens determined to give them a trial, and accordingly made an appointment to preach in a school-house in the neighborhood. The wicked inhabitants sent a message informing him that he should not preach, and if he made his appearance on that day they would mob him. As the time drew near his friends tried to dissuade him from his purpose, but he was resolved to fill his appointment or fail after every effort he was capable of making had been put forth. When the day arrived he took a few faithful friends and went to the school-house. When they arrived there they found the door locked and a large company of men, with a jug of whisky, in the yard. They threatened what they would do if he attempted to preach. Mr. Havens stepped upon a log near by and told them he had come to preach, and, by Divine assistance, intended to do so. He dared any of them to cross a pole which lay a little way in front of him till he invited them. He then announced the following text: "Yea, the light of the wicked shall be put out, and the spark of his fire shall not shine. The light shall be dark in his tabernacle, and his candle shall be put out with him. The steps of his strength shall be straitened, and his own counsel shall cast him down. For he is cast into a net by his own feet, and he walketh upon a snare. The gin shall take *him* by the heel, and the robber shall prevail against him. The snare *is* laid for him in the ground, and a trap for him in the way. Terrors shall make him afraid on every side, and shall drive him to his feet. His strength shall be hunger-bitten, and destruction *shall be* ready at his side." Job xviii, 5–12. While he poured out the terrors of the law not a man dared to move toward him, but many of them turned pale and stood trembling, while some wept freely. At the conclusion of his sermon he told them "if they desired to escape the damnation of hell, and would obtain mercy and pardon, and be prepared for heaven, to come and kneel down at the log upon which he stood and he would pray for them." Several came. His victory was complete.

We give another incident: In the bounds of a circuit which he traveled in Ohio, there lived a pious lady whose husband was so desperately wicked that he would not allow her to hold membership in any Church, nor suffer any minister to visit her. He owned a large farm and kept a distillery, employing many hands. He was a man of great muscular power, and was when enraged feared by most men. This pious lady's health declined till she was prostrated upon her bed. Mr. Havens desired to visit her, but his friends thought if he did he would get himself into trouble, and accomplish no good.

Reflecting upon the subject for some time, he felt it his duty to go, and resolved to make the attempt. His plan was to spend a night at her residence. He selected a friend to accompany him. They arrived at the place a little before the going down of the sun. He introduced himself to the lady, telling her who he was, and had some religious conversation with her. She expressed great gratification in seeing and enjoying with him a few minutes' conversation on the subject of religion, but said she could not invite him to stay all night, as her husband would not allow it. He told her to give herself no uneasiness on that subject, that he had come to stay all night and that he expected to do so.

He and his friend went out and put their horses in the stable, but did not venture to feed them. A little after dark the lady's husband came in with his hired hands from the farm. When he entered the room his wife introduced him to Mr. Havens. He immediately commenced abusing preachers, saying none had ever staid about his house, and never should. Mr. Havens informed him that he need feel no uneasiness on that account so far as he was concerned, that he had simply come in the discharge of his duty as a minister, to visit his sick wife. In a short time supper was announced in an adjoining room. This man and his hired men commenced gathering around the table, but no invitation was given to the visitors. Mr. Havens passed quickly into the room and took a seat at the table. As soon as he was seated he commenced asking a blessing. The landlord, who had not yet taken a seat, stood in amazement. While they were eating supper he continued his attacks upon religious people, particularly upon the Methodists, and *very* particularly upon Methodist preachers. Mr. Havens occasionally parried his thrusts. When supper was over, as they passed into the room where the sick woman lay, the husband said to Mr. Havens: "Well, you asked a blessing at my table, but you sha' n't pray in my house." He had no sooner spoken the words than Mr. Havens said, "Let us pray," and dropping upon his knees offered up a most earnest prayer, in which he presented the case of the sick lady, telling the Lord of her sufferings and trials, asking that grace might be vouchsafed unto her, and that God would have mercy upon her husband, and bless him and the children of the family. During the prayer the landlord stood aghast. At its conclusion he called his hired men and went off to the still-house.

Mr. Havens spent the evening till bedtime in religious conversation with the sick lady and her children. He and his friend were directed to lodge in a bedroom at the end of a long portico. Late in the night they heard the landlord with some of his hired men returning from the still-house. It was not long till they heard horses running in the barn-yard and dogs baying them. Mr. Havens said to his friend, "That fellow has turned our horses out of the stable, and is trying to dog them off. We must go and see to it." His friend pleaded to remain where they were—that it would be hazardous to go out, but he said, "No; we must go and see after them." They arose, and quickly dressing themselves went out to the barn-yard. Sure enough, the landlord was there hissing his dogs on their horses. Mr. Havens said to him, "Sir, what are you dogging our horses for?" The reply was, "You were too cursed lazy to feed them, and they have broken down my stable door and got out." "Very well," said Mr. Havens, "if that is all that is lacking we will attend to that now," and accordingly put them in the stable and gave them plenty of corn and hay. They then returned to the house and lay down again. The next morning they arose early and were preparing to depart when the landlord told them they could not leave till after breakfast. Said he, "You *would* stay all night, and you *would* pray, now you *shall* pray this morning, and have your breakfast before you go." They cheerfully consented.

Mr. Havens prayed with the family before breakfast, and when they were all seated at the table the landlord very politely invited him to ask a blessing. When they were about leaving the landlord said to Mr. Havens, "You are the only preacher that ever prayed in my house, or staid all night with me. Whenever you are passing this way call on me, and I will treat you like a gentleman." We give these incidents to show a prominent trait in Mr. Havens's character—a resolute will, a firmness of purpose to accomplish whatever he undertook.

He was a man of great power in prayer. Often while praying before preaching, Divine power so rested upon the congregation that sinners were made to tremble and the pious were filled with the love of God. He made it his rule to ask the Lord for whatever he needed. An incident occurred when he was preparing to enter the itinerancy which greatly encouraged him in all his after life to go to the Lord with all his wants. He was somewhat in debt, but had a sufficient amount in good promissory notes if he could cash them for any thing near what they called for to pay all his indebtedness. Times were hard and money scarce. There was but one man in all the region where he lived who paid cash for promissory notes. He was very wicked, and when he found a man in straitened circumstances he shaved him without stint, sometimes to half the amount of the face of the note. There was no alternative for Mr. Havens in raising the amount of money necessary to meet his indebtedness but to go to this extortioner. On his way he turned aside from the road, alighted from his horse, got down upon his knees and told the Lord his circumstances, that he was preparing to enter the itinerancy to call sinners to repentance; that he needed money to pay his debts, and earnestly besought him to soften the heart of the man to whom he was going, and influence him to let him have what money he needed at a reasonable per cent. When he reached the residence of the man he wished to see, he told him he was preparing for the itinerancy; that he had some good notes and wanted them cashed, as he was in need of money, and requested him to discount them as lightly as possible. The man took his notes, looked at them a moment, then went to his drawer, counted out the money and returned, saying, "Havens, I believe you are an honest man. You say you want to pay your debts and then go and preach. Here, I'll give you the face of your notes." And so he did, dollar for dollar.

Mr. Havens was particularly in his element when conducting the services at a camp meeting. On such occasions his great power over an audience, his ability to command were more fully developed. He was one of the best generals that ever took command of God's sacramental host on an encampment. When he had to come in contact with those who were disposed to violate the rules adopted for the government of such meetings, he never suffered a defeat. On one occasion, when he was holding a camp meeting on the southern border of Marion county, a huckster came and established himself with his commodities a short distance from the encampment, in violation of the law. Mr. Havens went to him and requested him to leave and go to a more remote distance, where he would not, by his traffic, produce disturbance. He refused to do so, and threatened if he was not let alone he would, with the whisky he had aboard, make drunk enough men to go to the encampment and drive the Methodists, preachers and people, from the ground. Mr. Havens left him and returned to the encampment, had the trumpet sounded and the people collected at the stand as quickly as possible. He told them what the huckster threatened to do, and called upon the young men in the audience to know if they were going to allow their mothers, wives, and sisters to be insulted and driven off the ground in that way. "No! no! no!" was responded from every part of the audience. One young man arose and said, " Mr. Havens, we will rout him. Come on, boys!" and, leading the way, some two hundred young men followed him. They proceeded to the huckster's establishment and informed him that he must leave immediately. He said "he reckoned not." They told him "it was even so." He proposed to go in a few hours. They said, "Now, immediately, or we will stamp your traps in the ground beneath our feet." They made him pack up and move *instanter*. They followed him some distance, and then warned him what the consequences would be in case he returned.

In fighting Satan at a camp meeting, if Mr. Havens did not succeed by one mode of attack he would change his tactics, and try another way. We give one instance: He was holding a camp meeting in Hamilton county. It had been in progress several days, but the Church had gained no decided victory. The camp-ground had been occupied for several years. Some of the meetings held there had not been very successful. Mr. Havens called "a council of war." He proposed to the preachers to fight the battle the approaching night upon new ground—not in the old altar. Said he, "We have fought the devil *there* till he understands that ground as well as we do; we will take him by surprise to-night." His plan of battle was agreed upon. The encampment was large, the tents inclosing much more space than was filled up with seats. He ordered several posts planted in the open space upon which to place lights, and a quantity of straw to be spread upon the ground where the light-posts stood, then a number of benches were brought and placed upon the straw. While these preparations were being made the people looked on with wonder and amazement. The inquiry was frequently made, "What does this mean? what are they going to do here?" but Mr. Havens and his preachers did not reveal the plan of battle. About the going down of the sun, he ordered prayer meetings commenced in various tents in different parts of the encampment, and appointed skillful men to lead them. After night had fully closed in, and while the prayer meetings were in full blast, he formed a circle of men joining hands around the light-posts and benches, directing them to admit no one within the circle but penitents, preachers, and such other persons as he might direct, and who would heartily enter into the spirit of the meeting.

He then appointed men to go to the different prayer meetings, and at the sound of the trumpet bring out the people and come sing to the circle, and if there were any penitents to bring them in and seat them upon the benches. By this time the excitement was running high. At the sound of the trumpet the people came in every direction from the prayer meetings, their songs rising and swelling, making the leaves upon the forest trees vibrate to the heavenly strains. The wicked were awestricken. Several penitents were brought inside the circle. Mr. Havens mounted a bench and gave an exhortation for burning pathos and moving power as seldom comes from the lips of man. At the conclusion, and while the congregation were singing that good old hymn, commencing,

"Come, ye sinners, poor and needy,"

some sixty or seventy weeping penitents crowded within the circle. The services continued till a late hour at night. Many souls were born of God, and the shout was heard afar off. The victory was complete. From this time the camp meeting went on gloriously. The next evening Mr. Havens said to the preachers, "We will fight the battle to-night in the old altar. The devil expects us to fight him up yonder where we did last night, but we will take him by surprise again."

Many incidents might be given showing different

traits in his character, but some of them have been published, and to give those that have not would extend this sketch beyond its proper limits.

His mind was vigorous and active—well-stored. His education was very limited when he entered the work of the ministry, but by industry and perseverance he acquired an extensive knowledge of men and things. He studied books closely. He was thoroughly acquainted with the standard writings in Methodist theology, and was well-skilled in using them. The Bible was his main book of study. He "searched the Scriptures" daily, and knew well how to handle the "Sword of the Spirit." He was a close student of men and things, and gathered a revenue from every thing around him. Few men were better judges of human nature than he. He could come as near forming a correct judgment of a man's character by closely scanning his countenance as any other person. Some very striking proofs of this might be given. He was of sanguine temperament, devoted in his friendship. His social qualities were of a high order. He possessed an almost inexhaustible fund of anecdote and repartee. Whoever undertook to break a lance with him in that way was very certain to come off second best. He had great compass of voice. It was soft and mellow in its tones till it became shattered by excessive labor. He knew well how to modulate it. He could throw it with great effect upon the ears of his hearers. He has frequently said he "thought he could tell when his voice hit the people" during the delivery of his sermons. He enjoyed the full confidence of his brethren in the ministry. He was three or four times elected delegate to the General Conference. The number of years he filled the important office of presiding elder shows to what extent he enjoyed the confidence of the appointing power.

As a preacher father Havens—for so he was called all the latter years of his life—stood in the first rank. He understood well the doctrines of the Methodist Episcopal Church, and was an able defender of them. He seldom failed, especially on popular occasions, to move and stir the souls of his audience to their very depths, and cause tears to flow in copious showers. His powers of declamation were of the highest order. Rev. Allen Wiley once said, "James Havens is the best declaimer I ever heard." He had a peculiar talent for presenting that which was awful. He frequently preached from such texts as, "Whatsoever thy hand findeth to do, do it with thy might; for there is no work, nor device, nor knowledge, nor wisdom, in the grave, whither thou goest;" and, "Woe to him that striveth with his Maker," and such subjects as led him to speak of the second coming of Christ, the resurrection, the destruction of the world, the day of judgment. But he did not present these alone. He loved to tell the story of the cross; to speak of the Christian's triumph in a dying hour; of the glories of heaven, and of saints robed in white, with harps in their hands. He had no stereotyped sermons. Though he used a text he had preached before, he always prepared a *new* sermon. He has, perhaps, preached to more people in Indiana than any other man. His faithful wife died a short time before his work was done, and left him to finish his journey alone. From the time of her death he never regained his former cheerfulness. Among the last acts of his ministerial life was to preach a sermon on Sunday, standing at the head of his wife's grave, with the Bible resting upon her tombstone, to a large and weeping audience.

After a painful and protracted illness, on the fourth day of November, 1864, in Rushville, he closed his eyes on all terrestrial things and opened them on the glories of heaven. He died in holy triumph, feeling that the Gospel he had preached to multiplied thousands in Indiana sustained and comforted him in a dying hour. His voice, which had fallen with so much melody upon the ears of listening thousands, is now forever hushed in death. Its trumpet tones shall no more be heard cheering on the faithful soldiers of the Cross, and inviting sinners to the Savior, crying, "Behold! behold the Lamb!" We see and hear him no more, but "his works do follow him." "He being dead, yet speaketh."

CHAPTER XXXIV.

REV. ISAAC OWEN.

THE subject of this sketch is worthy "to be had in everlasting remembrance," and will long live in the affections of those who knew him. The more intimately he was known, the more highly was he appreciated. He was not so attractive at first sight, but as your acquaintance ripened he would draw you close and closer to himself.

Isaac Owen was born in Wilton, Vermont, March 8, 1809. In 1811 he was brought by his parents to Indiana, then a Territory. His father settled in the woods in Knox county. Like most of the early emigrants, he was poor; hence he could not make extensive provision for the comfort of his family. This subjected Isaac as he grew up to many hardships and privations. To be the son of a poor man in a wilderness country did not bode a bright future. As an instance of the hardships and privations to which his father's family were subjected, we give the following as related by Mr. Owen in after years: "When I was a boy we lived in the woods, in Knox county. Grist mills were few and far between. In order to get meal to make our bread we had to pound the corn in a hominy mortar, with a pestle. In the Winter season, sometimes having no shoes, I was driven to the expedient of heating blocks of wood to stand upon, in order to keep my bare feet from the frozen ground, while I pounded the corn to make meal for our bread."

In 1824 his father fell a victim to the disease and exposures incident to a new country, leaving him with his widowed mother to struggle with all the infelicities of poverty. She had early sown the good seed in his tender mind, and had daily carried him in the arms of faith and prayer before the throne of Heavenly mercy. And now, being left a widow, all the care of her children devolving upon herself, with greater earnestness she besought the widows' God to lead her children "to the Rock that was higher than they." It was not long till her prayers in Isaac's behalf were answered. In the sixteenth year of his age he was converted and joined the Methodist Episcopal Church. Boy though he was, he took up the cross and began to pray in public. Continuing faithful, growing in grace and in the knowledge of Divine things, he was, after a time, licensed to preach. This laid upon him a burden which was hard to bear; nevertheless, throwing himself upon the Lord, he found grace to enable him to stand in his lot. In the Fall of 1834 he was admitted on trial in the Indiana Conference, and sent to Otter Creek mission.

Mr. Owen's early opportunities to obtain an education were poor, but possessing great energy of character he applied himself to study with diligence, using the facilities he had to the best advantage. At the end of two years he was received into full connection in the Conference and ordained deacon, and at the end of four years graduated to elder's orders.

Though he traveled hard circuits for several years, he continued to apply himself closely to study. When he had pretty thoroughly mastered the English grammar, he commenced the study of the Greek language, which he continued to pursue till he obtained a fair knowledge thereof. While engaged in his literary pursuits he did not neglect the study of theology, but divided his time between his literary and theological studies. He attained quite an eminence as a theologian.

As a preacher he was plain, clear, logical, and forcible, always shedding light upon the subject he had in hand. Though not an orator, he seldom failed to make an impression upon his hearers, and often moved his congregation to tears. His delivery was good, his voice pleasant. He had an inventive genius, full of expedients, ready for any emergency. As an evidence of this we give one instance. When he was a boy some twelve years old, the country new, the forest dense, the population sparse, he went into the woods one day in search of some missing cattle. Traveling in various directions, he lost his course and became bewildered, so that he could not tell in which direction his home was. For an hour or two he strove to right himself, but all in vain. He was still lost. The sun was getting low, night would soon close in—something had to be done. The faithful old family dog was with him. Believing the dog knew the course home, he hit upon the following expedient. Having cut a switch he called the dog to him, took hold of him, gave him a good basting and then let him go. The dog bounded away through the thick woods, and the boy after him at the top of his speed. The dog soon distanced him and was out of sight, but Isaac kept on the course the dog had gone, and about dark arrived safely at his father's cabin.

Mr. Owen was original in preaching—he did not allow himself to use skeletons prepared by other men. He selected his texts and then prepared his sermons on the texts. He did not *first* make his sermon and then search for a text to suit it. He had a strong, clear, discriminating mind, and could look into a passage of Scripture and soon see the points to be presented to the congregation. He had a peculiar faculty for raising money for Church purposes. His great success was not so much before a public congregation as by personal application. If he called upon a man for a contribution and he declined to give, the more he declined the more Owen good-naturedly pressed his plea. If the man became surly or crusty Owen was the more bland and pleasant. He seldom failed to obtain a contribution if he called upon a man.

He was one of the four agents first sent out to

raise an endowment-fund for Indiana Asbury University. To say he was successful in his agency would be to say what is well known to the friends of the institution in its early history. He served in the agency four years, and in that time succeeded in raising, by the sale of perpetual scholarships, about sixty-three thousand dollars. He did more to build up Indiana Asbury University, financially, by raising funds, than any other man.

He labored fourteen years in Indiana as an itinerant. In 1848 he was appointed one of the first missionaries to California, and in the Spring of 1849 crossed the plains with his family. Soon after reaching California, and before he had commenced housekeeping, he lost all his personal goods by the sinking of a steamer. This left him in great destitution, a stranger in a strange land. But, nothing daunted or discouraged, he went to work, trusting in his Divine Master. He was the first man appointed to the presiding eldership in California.

In physical stature Mr. Owen was of medium size, well-proportioned. He had a finely-formed head, inclining to baldness, hair dark, a well-developed forehead, piercing black eyes, a dimple in one cheek, a well-curved mouth, and always wore a pleasant smile. He was affable, social, kind in his disposition, and affectionate. As descriptive of the latter part of Mr. Owen's life, and of the final closing scene, we take the following from a funeral discourse preached before the California Conference by

Rev. John Daniel: "The following shows that amid his many cares and labors his mind was dwelling on the final conflict: 'I keep death before me. I regard it a mere question of time and as the end of toil, the end of care. My time in this world is growing short. I hope to be able to improve the few hours I may enjoy as so many precious hours of probation, and to honor Christ my Savior and Redeemer.'

"Again: 'I feel that my time for improvement in this world is short, yet I am as strong for all the duties of my office as I was years ago. My great desire is to finish life with life's labors. The thought of being put on the retired list is horrible to me. Let me cease to work and live the same day.'

"His death was in near accordance with his wishes. What seemed at first to be a trivial accident to his hand had proved the cause of great suffering and physical prostration. On coming home from the Santa Cruz quarterly meeting, he could scarcely retain his place in the saddle, and had to be assisted from his horse. The brethren in San Francisco, the place of his next meeting, learning of his prostrate condition, kindly sent word that they would excuse him, while all pecuniary requirements should be met and attended to as if he were there. But he could not be prevailed on to rest. He went to the city, and on Friday morning filled an appointment at Oakland, returning in the afternoon. In the evening, having an appointment in the Folsom-Street German Church, he went, and though not able to preach, delivered an address to those present, and conducted the business of the quarterly conference as usual. This was his last public service. He grew worse, retired to the parsonage in connection with the church of his last service, where he lingered till Friday, February 9, at one o'clock, when he quietly fell asleep. In his last moments he had the soothing attentions of his wife and kind ministerial brethren, together with the best medical aid. His ruling passion of life—to labor for the Church—was manifest in his affliction, but it was in harmony with the will of God. His words in the brief period of his last illness were free, but they were in unison with his life and with his sacred calling. To one he spoke of how delightful it would be to go and enjoy the Christian's reward. When desired to try and get rest, he said, 'I shall soon be at rest.' To a brother minister he said, 'The waves are dashing around me, but I have measured the depth of the waters; they will waft me to a peaceful shore.' Again he said, 'The river is cold, and deep, and calm.'"

Thus passed away our beloved brother Owen after nearly thirty-two years uninterrupted employment in the vineyard of the Lord. Industry, zeal, and faithfulness marked his life; resignation, serenity, and hope in his dying hours. Heaven's holy rest, the Savior's glory, is the unending reward.

CHAPTER XXXV.

EDWARD BROWN.

THE subject of this sketch having emigrated to Indiana at an early day labored faithfully in the Redeemer's cause, wielding an extensive influence for good, and having maintained a high reputation for moral integrity, is worthy to be remembered, and deserves a permanent record.

Edward Brown was born in Baltimore county, Maryland, June 7, 1774. When a small child he was brought by his parents to the State of Ohio. In his youth he returned to Baltimore county, where he served an apprenticeship. When fully grown to manhood, he was united in marriage to Miss Elizabeth Kemp, a young lady well qualified to be a "help-meet" for him. Soon after his marriage with his wife he went to the city of Baltimore, where he took up his residence. He continued to reside in the city till September, 1819, when, with his family, he started for the then Far West. On the seventh day of December following, he arrived in New Albany, Indiana, then a small town on the Ohio River. Here he resided to the close of his life, a period of thirty-six years. Father Brown—as he was familiarly called all the latter years of his life—was of medium hight, with a well-proportioned physical frame. His neck was short, face broad, mouth wide, nose prominent, forehead well developed, hair black, parted upon the top of his head, and falling down to his shoulders. His countenance indicated great firmness and decision of character. His appearance was intellectual. In the prime of life his walk was erect and his step firm.

He was converted in the seventeenth year of his age, alone in the woods, while engaged in prayer. The evidence of his conversion was so clear and satisfactory that he never afterward doubted that God did, for Christ's sake, then and there pardon his sins. His soul was filled unutterably full of joy. He soon told his friends what great things the Lord had done for him. He did not connect himself with any branch of the Church till 1804, when he joined the Methodist Episcopal Church in the city of Baltimore. From that time to the end of his life his attachment to the Church of his choice increased in strength; and though many of his friends—among them his brother, Rev. George Brown, D. D.—went off with those who formed the Methodist Protestant Church, he remained firm in his adherence to the old Church. Such were his talents, religious zeal, steadfastness, and upright walk from the time he united with the Church that he soon became a prominent member. He was an intimate friend of Bishop George, and was one of the pall-bearers at the Bishop's funeral. While residing in the city of Baltimore he was licensed to officiate in the Church as an exhorter, which relation he retained through life. He was a member of the first class organized in New Albany, and was also a member of the first boards of stewards and trustees organized in the place. These offices he filled with great acceptability and usefulness, ever watchful of the interest and welfare of his pastor, the poor, and the Church; and when, from infirmity, he could no longer serve actively in these offices, his brethren continued him in them as a token of respect for his past services.

As a steward he was a safe counselor of the pastor, ever attentive to the wants of his family, making it his rule to visit them once or twice every week to see if they needed any thing for their comfort. As trustee he was faithful in discharging the duties of that important office, looking well to the comfort of the congregation when assembled for worship. As an exhorter he was not showy, but impressive. Understanding well the doctrines of the Methodist Episcopal Church, he never inculcated error. He was gifted in prayer, and always prayed with great fervency of spirit. He had strong confidence in the efficacy of prayer. Having been converted while wrestling with the Lord in prayer, he delighted to pray with penitents at the altar. Many precious souls have been "brought out of darkness into the marvelous light," while father Brown was presenting their cause before the blood-besprinkled throne. Being "diligent in business," he accumulated a very handsome property, which he used to the glory of God, giving liberally to the support of the Church and all benevolent institutions. He was plain in his apparel, wearing the old-fashioned round-breasted Methodist coat, and broad-brimmed drab hat. He was a great enemy to pride, and was faithful in his testimony against it when and wherever he thought he saw it developed, in the Church or out of it, in preachers or private members. He was opposed to church-steeples with bells hung in them, to gayety in the apparel of the members of the Church, jewelry, vails, ruffles, and artificial flowers; to ministers wearing their beard. All these he believed to be the developments of pride, and, as he often expressed it, "came from the devil and would go to the devil." He was very decidedly opposed to the use of a richly-decorated hearse, with its nodding plumes, and the great display often made on funeral occasions in cities. He believed them to be displays of vanity, and evil in their tendency, often causing families to expend an amount of money to keep up appearances on these solemn occasions they were not able to afford.

He repeatedly made the request of his friends that when he should die his body should not be placed in a *hearse* to be conveyed to the grave; that there should be no display of carriages in his funeral procession, saying, "When I die I want to be carried to the grave on the shoulders of my friends, all the people marching on foot. If I have not friends enough to carry me to the grave, put me upon a dray. Don't let my body go into a *hearse*." Some may think that in all this father Brown was governed by a prejudice which was the result of a lack of refined cultivation, but such was not the fact. All who knew him awarded to him honesty and Christian candor in his opposition to whatever he believed to be the result of pride. He was a faithful witness for Jesus, ever ready to testify that " Christ has power on earth to forgive sins; that the blood of Jesus can cleanse from all sin; that perfect love casteth out all fear that hath torment." In 1841 the wife of his youth was taken from him by death. This he felt to be a sore trial, but grace sustained him. After the death of his wife he found a home with his son-in-law and daughter, Mr. and Mrs. Beeler, who kindly administered to his comfort as the infirmities of advanced age came upon him. As he drew near the close of life his soul ripened for the heavenly garner, death lost all its terror, and the grave its gloom. He looked forward to the moment of his departure with great delight. A few days before his death he went to the undertaker and selected a plain coffin, in which he wished to sleep his last long sleep, and had it set aside till it should be needed. He then went to the city cemetery and pointed out to the sexton the precise spot in his own family lot where he wished to be buried, saying, "There I want my body to rest till the resurrection morn." The evening before he was attacked with his death sickness he led the family devotion. He was unusually drawn out in prayer. In his petitions he embraced all the Churches, particularly the one in which he had so long lived and labored. He was greatly blessed. In the morning he was very ill. His sickness was of short duration. In the afternoon of March 16, 1855, he finished his earthly pilgrimage, in the eighty-second year of his age, having been a member of the Church fifty-one years. In accordance with his request his remains were carried on a *bier*, the oldest citizens of New Albany serving as pall-bearers, to Wesley Chapel, where a funeral discourse was delivered to a large congregation from Hebrews xi, 14. At the close of the sermon the procession formed, all marching on foot to the grave, where the funeral services were read. Father Brown lived a long life of earnest, consistent piety, and died respected by all who knew him.

CHAPTER XXXVI.

REV. CALVIN W. RUTER.

ALL the efforts I have made to obtain information in regard to Mr. Ruter's early life; the place of his birth; his training in childhood and youth; when and where he was converted and united with the Church, etc., have been unsuccessful. In attempting to write a sketch of him I am well aware I can not do justice to his memory, or present such a portrait of him as his great worth demands; nevertheless, as he was so prominently connected with the planting of Methodism in the State, and did so much to lay the foundation of the Church deep and broad, I can not consent to pass him by unnoticed, for he was, in the language of Rev. D. M'Intire, in a letter now before me, "one of the apostles of Methodism in Indiana." As a tribute to the memory of an able minister of the Lord Jesus this brief sketch is presented, leaving to others who knew him better, and who wield an abler pen, to write more at large.

Calvin W. Ruter was born in one of the New England States some time in the year 1790. In youth he came to the State of Ohio. His surroundings were such as to throw him principally upon his own resources, which tended much to his development, physically and mentally. In early manhood he performed some hard manual labor. Having been converted, and having united with the Methodist Episcopal Church, he was licensed to preach, and, according to the bound "Minutes of the Several Annual Conferences," he was received on trial in the Ohio Conference in the Fall of 1818. His first appointment was to Steubenville circuit, with Samuel Hamilton and William Knox for his colleagues, he being the junior preacher. At the close of his second year in the Conference, in the Fall of 1820, he was admitted into full connection, ordained deacon, and transferred to the Missouri Conference, which embraced all of Indiana except Whitewater, Lawrenceburg, and Madison circuits. Mr. Ruter was appointed to Silver Creek circuit as preacher in charge, with Job Baker for his colleague. This was his introduction into the work in Indiana. The circuit was large, covering the territory known as "Clark's Grant." On this circuit he emphatically made his mark, planting the Church in some localities where it still continues to flourish and grow. Samuel Hamilton, who had been his colleague on his first circuit in Ohio, where their hearts had been knit together like those of David and Jonathan, was now his presiding elder. This year a camp meeting was held in the bounds of the circuit, superintended by Hamilton, the presiding elder, and Ruter, the preacher in charge. The following account of that camp meeting is taken from a sketch written by Rev. W. H. Goode, of North Indiana Conference, which now lies before me: "This camp meeting was held, perhaps, in October. . . . One morning, looking out from their tents, they discovered the whole face of the earth covered with snow. [Rather chilling we should say to their prospects.] But these men of God were nothing daunted, and the tent-holders, too, were no fair-weather Christians. The people hungered for the Bread of Life; souls were *there* to be saved; firmly they maintained their post in prayer and supplication. God looked down upon the scene. The sun melted away the snow, and the Word of God melted the hearts of the people. A Pentecostal scene ensued. Souls in large numbers were converted—the neighborhood was revolutionized. Almost half a century has passed and still one of the leading country churches of Southern Indiana marks the spot. Many an aged pilgrim, the steadfast fruit of that revival, is still on the way, surrounded by a godly household of the second and third generations. Some half a dozen of the converts entered the Christian ministry."

Mr. Ruter continued to reside and labor in Indiana to the close of his useful life. He was, through failing health, at different times compelled to take a superannuated relation to his Conference; but was, when his health would allow it, found in the effective ranks. He filled some of the most important stations as pastor, and was for several years presiding elder. He enjoyed the confidence of his brethren in the ministry in a high degree, and was, by them, elected three or four times to represent them in the General Conference of the Church. He was a member of the General Conference of 1844, which met in the city of New York, when the celebrated cases of Bishop Andrew and Rev. Francis A. Harding came before that body. During his superannuation he filled several offices of public trust honorably and acceptably to the people. He was postmaster in the city of New Albany for four years under the administration of President Polk, after which he held the office of Register of the Land-Office, at Indianapolis, for four years. He did not allow these offices to interfere with his attachment to the Church, nor his devotion to her interests. Though superannuated he took a lively interest in every thing that pertained to the prosperity of Zion, and preached as often as his health would allow. He was a man of fine appearance, having a physical frame about six feet in hight, well-proportioned, and a finely-developed forehead. He was always dignified, and would, by his lofty bearing, attract attention in any company or deliberative body. Any one looking upon his noble form would have been impressed that he was a man of much more than ordinary intellect and talents. His education was fair—above mediocrity. His administrative abilities were of the first class. He was cautious, mild, prudent, firm. He understood well the Discipline of the Church. His talents as a preacher were of a high order. His voice was pleasant, and at times of great compass. He knew well how to use it. He could tell an incident with great effect. In his sermons he was very pathetic, and often moved his audience to tears. When in his full vigor few men were more successful in preaching on popular occasions, such as camp meetings and quarterly meetings. On camp meeting occasions he was a good commander, knowing well how to direct the battle and use the forces he had to the best advantage. Rev. W. H. Goode, in his sketch from which we have already quoted, speaking of Mr. Ruter as a preacher, says: "His preaching was plain, clear, lucid; always making out fairly what he took in hand; sound in theology and rich in Christian experience, as well as eminently practical. But his great strength lay in his *pathos* and the melting appeals that often closed his discourses. These were, at times, overpowering, especially at camp meetings and on popular occasions. At such times he ordinarily left the pulpit broken down, prostrate in bodily strength; but brought down the 'pillars' of the temple with him." As a friend Mr. Ruter was kind, generous, and true. Rev. J. A. Brouse, of the South-Eastern Indiana Conference, in a communication which now lies before me, says: "My acquaintance with brother Ruter commenced in the

Fall of 1832, which continued till his death. From the time of our first acquaintance we kept up a regular correspondence. We have been associated together in the work of the ministry. He has been my presiding elder, and I have been his. In all these relations I ever found him a confidential friend and safe adviser." The exact date of his death is not now known to the writer, but was about 1859. He died on Saturday, in the afternoon, at his residence near Patriot, in Switzerland county. He had preached a sermon in the forenoon characterized by his usual power and efficiency. In the afternoon, while engaged in shaving himself, he was attacked by his old enemy, the heart disease, and fell upon the floor a corpse. Thus passed away this distinguished minister of the Lord Jesus. In the morning of his last day on earth he cried, "Behold! behold the Lamb!" and in the afternoon fell asleep in Jesus. He and his compeers, Strange, Hamilton, Wiley, Havens, and Armstrong, are now together around the throne.

THE END.

Index

----, Charlie 227 228
    Edwin 156 George
    135 James 272
    Lucien 246 Mr 191
    Patience 158 Rachel
    158 Russel 190
A, B 18 Miss 214 Mr
    240 241
ABBOTT, Benjamin
    162
ABRAMS, Israel 68
ADAMS, John Quincy
    118
ANDERSON, D 115
    Daniel 113 114
    David 112
ANDREW, Bishop 302
ARMSTRONG, 304
    James 109-115
AXLEY, James 55 Mr
    55

B, Mr 92
BAKER, Henry 108 109
    Job 108 300 Job M
    109 110 John M
    109
BASCOM, Henry B 267
    Mr 268
BASSET, Samuel 113
BAUGHMAN, 175 John
    A 173 Mr 173-175
BEAUCHAMP, William
    110
BECK, Asa 172
BEECHER, Henry
    Ward 253
BEELER, Mr 297 Mrs
    297
BEESLY, 26
BEGGS, Mr 168 177
    Rev Mr 169 S R 114
    115 Stephen R 110

BEGGS (Cont.)
  113 167 177
BENSON, 141
BERRY, 246-248 251
  252 258 Dr 254-
  257 259-265 L W
  260 264 Lucien W
  262 Lucien William
  246 Mr 250-253
  Mrs 249
BIGELOW, 132 Margaret 187 Mr 166 188-190 192 193 Russel 60 66 110 166 176 185 190 191 193 197
BIGGS, Jane 25
BLACKMAN, Learner 54 Mr 54
BRADLEY, Brother 262
BROOKS, Brother 261 Joseph 260
BROUSE, J A 303
BROWN, Edward 293 Elizabeth 293 Father 293 295 297 298 George 294 Samuel 108
BUELL, Henry 114 115
BURKE, William 150 52 54
BURNES, Robert 114 115

C, Mr 23 92 W 89 91 92
CAIN, Hardy 100 John 66
CALHOUN, John C 118
CAMPBELL, Alexander 250
CARTWRIGHT, Peter 57
CHAMBERLIN, Daniel 109 David 109
CHAMBERS, 40 Mrs 40
CHAPMAN, 120-123 Joseph 119 120
CHEEVER, Abner H 114
CHEVER, A H 115
CHRISTIE, Mr 246 247 W B 246
CLARKE, 141 Dr 141
CLAY, Henry 118
COFFMAN, 24
COLLARD, James 108
COLLINGS, Henry 25 Jane 25 John 25 Lydia 25 Mr 25 Mrs Henry 25 Mrs Richard 25 Richard 25 William 25 Zebulon 25
CONNELL, Zachariah 107

CORD, John 60 107
   109-113
COX, Jeremiah 165
CRAVENS, William 109
   110
CRAWFORD, Josiah 51
   Thomas H 118
CRISS, 40
CRUME, 131 Moses 51
   54 58 60 65 107
   145 197 Mr 54 146
CULL, Father 159 161
   Hugh 49 74 157
   161 Mr 158 159
   Rachel 157
CUMMINS, 110 131 A
   187 Alexander 66
   109
DALLY, 204
DANIEL, Joseph 291
DAVIS, Thomas 59 60
   114 115
DILLON, 24
DIXON, William 56
DODDRIDGE, 102 103
   John 102 103 Mr
   102 103
DURBIN, John P 108
E, Mr 214 230
EDGE, Benjamin 55
ELLIOTT, Arthur W 66
   108 C 261

EMMONS, 250 F W
   250 251 Mr 250
EPPERSON, 234 James
   224-226 229 233
   235 Mr 226-233
   235 Mrs 227 234
EVANS, William 115
EVERHART, John 110
   239 Mr 240 241
EVERHEART, John
   108
FARMER, E P 115 Eli P
   113
FAY, Adaline 249
FERNANDES, Henry S
   108
FIEHRER, Elaine 13
FILES, Thomas 114
   115
FINLEY, 131 J B 190
   James B 56 266 Mr
   190 266 Robert W
   55 56
FISH, John 111
FISHER, Orseneth 112
   114
FLETCHER, 141
FLINT, Mrs 40
FRALY, Daniel 41 59
FULTON, Elisha W 170
   68 Mr 68
G, A M C 242 Brother

G (Cont.)
   243 Mr 242-245
GARNER, James 111
   114 115
GATCH, George 110
   188
GEORGE, Bishop 294
GIBSON, John 162 163
   Mr 163
GLAIZE, Samuel 109
GOODE, W H 301 303
GRIFFITH, 132 Mr
   206-209 N B 111
   114 115 Nehemiah
   B 110 113 208
   Walter 55 56 66
   108
H, 210 J 210 J 222 Mr
   182 211 212 214-
   223 28 Mrs 28 29
   177-179 181 183
   223
HALE, Jesse 107 111
HAMILTON, 110 300
   304 Samuel 108
   109 300
HARDING, Francis A
   302
HARDY, Brother 262
   John 115
HARGRAVE, Richard
   111-113 208

HARRISON, Charles 58
   Gen 53 119 Gov 53
   William H 53
HATHAWAY, Father
   145
HAVENS, 264 284 304
   Anna 266 David
   266 George 266
   James 66 67 111-
   115 166 257 264
   265 269 284 John
   265 Landy 266 Mr
   68 270 271 273-
   282 Mrs 266 Nancy
   265
HENRY, James 170 Mr
   171
HENSON, Thomas 113
HESTER, G K 111
   George K 109-111
   113 George V 109
HEWSON, Thomas 110
   111
HIGGENBOTHAM,
   Anna 266
HITT, T S 115 Thomas
   S 111 113
HOGAN, John 114
HOLLIDAY, Charles 58
   113-115 F C 196
HONLEY, James 100
HOOVER, David 236

HORN, George 111
HUDSON, 27 Mr 27-29
    Mrs 27 28
HULL, Samuel 111 112
HUNT, William 59 60
INDIAN, Green 32 33
    Killbuck 21 22 Old
    Sal 22
INGERSOLL, John 110
IRWIN, Margaret 187
J, J 89 91
JACKSON, Andrew 118
    Gen 119 Isaac 166
JAYNES, John 110
JOCELYN, Augustus
    66
JOHNSON, John T 114
JONES, 29 30 C B 115
    James 108 109 111
    113 66 Mrs 29
JULIAN, 96 97 George
    94 Mr 95
K, A 242 Brother 243
    244 Mr 169 242
    243 Mrs 168 169
KEMP, Elizabeth 293
KENNEDY, Sarah 136
KENT, John T 107
KING, Thomas A 59
KINKADE, Joseph 109
    59
KNOX, William 300

LANGDON, Solomon
    54 55
LAWRENCE, Benjamin
    60 107 108
LINDSEY, Isaac 54
LOCK, George 113-115
LOW, S 115 Samuel
    111 113 114
M, Mr 221
M'CORD, James 60
    John 60
M'CUEN, 251 252 Mr
    253
M'DOWEL, Brother 261
    J 247 J W 261 Mr
    247
M'HENRY, Daniel 60
    107 108
M'INTIRE, D 299
M'KEAN, James 115
M'MEHAN, William 55
M'REYNOLDS, J W 115
    William 110
MADISON, 111
MAVITY, William 107
    115
MEDFORD, William
    107 111
MEEK, Rachel 157
MILLER, Charles W
    101 John 111-113
    115 Mr 101

MOORE, William 112 114 115
MORGAN, 26 27
　Charles 26
MORRIL, John 25 Mrs 25 Mrs John 25
MORRIS, Bishop 55 56 262
MURRY, James 109 110
MYERS, Jacob 225 Mr 225 226
NELSON, 52 Thomas 51 57 74
NEWTON, D 115
　Daniel 114
NOBLE, James 96
NORRIS, Capt 25 John 25
ODELL, Patsy 81
OTWELL, S M 115
　Stith M 114
OWEN, 289 292 Isaac 286 Mr 286 287 289 290
OWENS, 96
PAIN, Sela 52
PARKER, Mr 51
　Samuel 50 52
PAYNE, Jeremiah 24 25 Mrs 25
PENN, William 135

PERKINS, James H 13
PIERSON, Mrs 166
　Widow 166
PITT, 86 87
POLK, President 302
POWNAL, John 107
　Joseph 108
POWNEL, Joseph 60
QUIN, William P 108 109
RANDLE, George 112-114
RAPER, W H 110 William H 108 206
RARIDEN, James 236 Mr 237-241 Mrs 238
RAWSON, Silas 175
RAY, Edwin 112-115 156 Gov 97 James B 97
RICE, Thomas 110
RICHARDS, Richard 57
RISLEY, Ashley 115
ROBINSON, Mr 172 174 R S 207 Richard S 172 Smith L 114
RODDY, 86 87 Christopher 84 Mr 84 85
RUARK, Shadrach 59
RUCKLE, John G 256

RUE, Esquire 30
RUTER, 300 303
  Calvin 108-110
  Calvin W 114 299
  Mr 299-301 303
  S, 231 Brother 244
  245 Mr 216-222
  Rev Mr 194 Sister
  233
SALE, John 49 51 74
  107
SANFORD, H 146
  Hector 51 145
SCOTT, James 110
  114 115
SCRIPPS, John 59 109
SHANKS, William 113-
  115
SHARP, David 58 59
  107
SHAW, Jonathan 26
SHRADER, John 59 60
  108 109
SIMPSON, Dr 253
SLOCUM, Charles 115
SLOCUMB, Charles 60
SMITH, Edward 111
  112 G C 125 George
  30 51 78 126 135
  166 John 165
  Mercy B 166 Mrs 79
  80 125 Rachel S
  166 Sarah 125 166

SMITH (Cont.)
  W C 143 W H 115
  William B 114
  William H 112
STEPHENS, Benjamin
  115 Peter 111
STEWART, J 110 John
  108 109
STILWELL, Thomas 54
STONE, Elias 109
STRANGE, 131 304
  John 56 59 66 110
  111 113-115 148
  154 156 Mr 148-
  153 155
SUMMERVILLE, John
  66
T, C 88 91
TALBERT, Othniel 60
TARKINGTON, Joseph
  114
TAYLOR, James C 110
  Rev Mr 154
TEST, John 238 Miss
  238
THOMAS, Margaret
  166 Stephen 166
THOMPSON, 52 Bishop
  193 Edward 185 J L
  115 James L 109
  110 111 113 114
  Mr 52 Samuel H 51
  60 74 111 114

TURNER, James 55
VARNER, Jacob 111
VREDENBURG, H 113 208
WALKER, Jesse 58 59
WALLACE, John 107-109
WALPOLE, 120-123 Thomas 120
WARE, James 55
WEBSTER, Ebenezer 109 Ebenezer T 110
WELLS, James T 109
WESLEY, 129 141
WEST, Asa D 114 Samuel 60
WHITE, Levi 110
WILEY, 132 304 Allen 60 66 107-109 111 113-115 187 196 202 207 258 284 Mr 196 197 199 200 203 204
WILLEY, Dennis 110 111
WILLIAM, Mr 49
WILLIAMS, Joseph 49 Mr 50 Rev Mr 145
WILLIFORD, William L 30
WINANS, Mr 52 53 William 52
WITTEN, Zachariah 58
WOOD, Aaron 110 111 114 E G 207 Enoch G 115
WRIGHT, John F 110
YOUNG, Jacob 55 158

www.ingramcontent.com/pod-product-compliance
Lightning Source LLC
Chambersburg PA
CBHW070723160426
43192CB00009B/1287